Mel Bay Presents
Mastering the Guitar 1B
A COMPREHENSIVE METHOD FOR TODAY'S GUITARIST!

By William Bay &
Mike Christiansen

W9-BAL-188

CONTENTS

Available in 2002 to supplement this series:

Jazz Theory Handbook — book/CD set

Guitar Workbook/Learning Guitar Fingerboard Theory — book

Mastering the Guitar Class Method/Elementary to 8th Grade Level — book & 2-CD set

Mastering the Guitar Class Method/Beginning-9th Grade and Higher — book & 2-CD set

Mastering the Guitar/Teacher's Supplement (Level 1 & 2) — books

Mastering the Guitar Class Method (Levels 1 & 2) — books & CDs

Mastering the Guitar Lesson Plans (Levels 1 & 2) — books

Mastering the Guitar Ensembles (Levels 1 & 2) — books

Mastering the Guitar Theory Workbook/Test Booklet (Levels 1 & 2) — books

Mastering the Guitar/Level 2 — CD set

Stringing the Guitar Chart — chart

2 3 4 5 6 7 8 9 0

Sixteenth Notes

A sixteenth note looks like this: ♪ It gets ¼ beat, if the bottom number in the time signature is 4.

Several sixteenth notes together look like this: or

A sixteenth rest looks like this:

It takes two sixteenth notes to equal one eighth note, or four sixteenth notes to equal one quarter note.

Table of Notes and Rests

Whole Note	o	Whole Measure Rest
Half Notes		Half Rest
Quarter Notes		Quarter Rest
Eighth Notes		Eighth Rest
Sixteenth Notes		Sixteenth Rest

Counting Sixteenth Notes

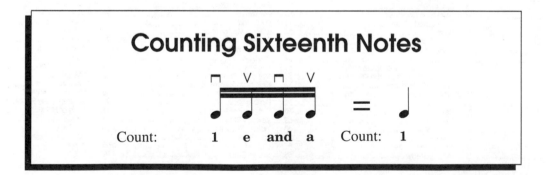

Study

Solos

CD #1
Track #1

Fingerstyle or Flatpick Solo
Moderately slow, gently

Sea Breeze

WB

CD #1
Track #2

Flatpick Solo
Moderately

Cumberland Trail

WB

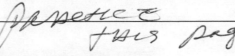

CD #1
Track #3

Wellsville Ridge

For a review of 2/4 time, see page 7.

Flatpick Solo
Moderate, walking tempo

MC

8th and Two 16ths

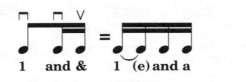

1   and &   1 (e) and a

Count: **1   & a 2   & a 3   & a 4   & a**

CD #1
Track #4

What Shall We Do with the Drunken Sailor?

Flatpick Solo

Sea Chanty

Island Fever

Reggae Jam

Waly, Waly

16th Notes

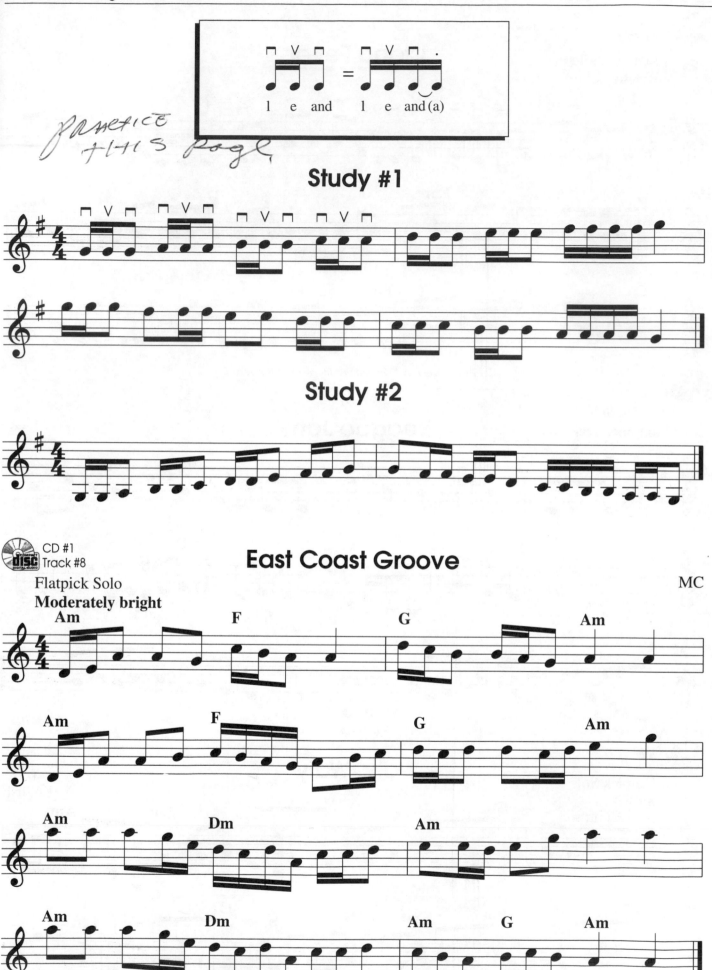

PRACTICE THIS PAGE.

Study #1

Study #2

CD #1
Track #8

East Coast Groove

Flatpick Solo

MC

Moderately bright

Am   F   G   Am

Am   F   G   Am

Am   Dm   Am

Am   Dm   Am   G   Am

16th Notes

CD #1
Track #9

Flatpick Solo
Easy blues feel

West Side Blues

MC

Sixteenth Note Triplets

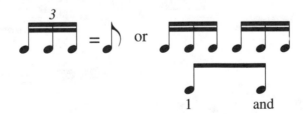

1   and

²⁄₄ Time Review

In **²⁄₄** time, we have 2 beats to the measure. A quarter note gets one beat.

16th Notes

CD #1
Track #10

The Downfall of Paris

WB
Set Dance

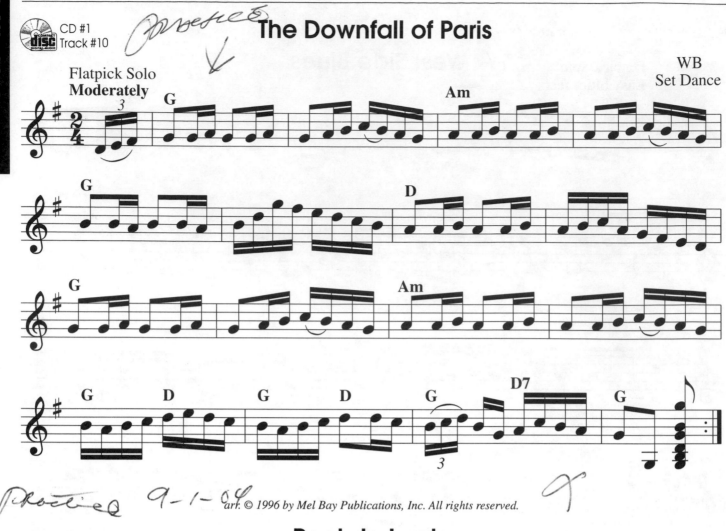

Reel de Lapin

CD #1
Track #11

WB
French Canadian

16th Notes

9-14-04

The Lily of the Valley

WB
Bluegrass Gospel

Flatpick Solo
Moderately, with a beat
Acc. Chords

Flatpicking Solo

9-21-04

Drowsy Maggie

Flatpick Solo
Lively tempo
Acc. Chords

WB
Irish

16th Notes

Dotted Eighths and Sixteenths

A dotted eighth note followed by a sixteenth note is a common figure in music. Practice the following study until it is felt and understood.

Study #1

Slowly

All are Played the same

Study #2

Count: 1   a 2   a 3   a 4   a 1   a 2   a 3 e & a 4

Study #3

CD #1
Track #14

The Keel Row

WB
English Sea Song

Flatpick Solo
Rhythmically

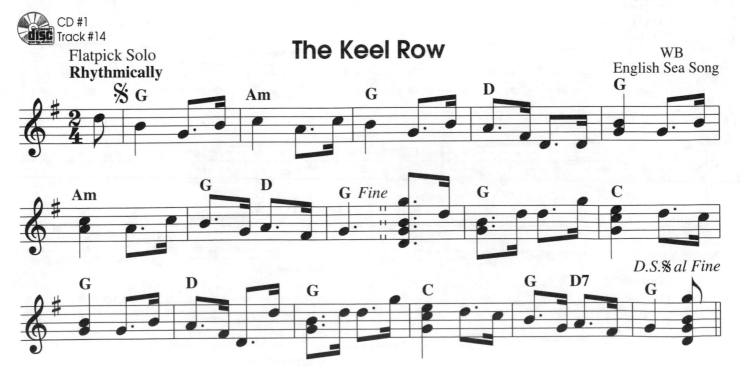

arr. © 1996 by Mel Bay Publications, Inc. All rights reserved.

CD #1
Track #15

10-5-04

Loch Lomond

WB
Scotland

Flatpick Solo
Slowly

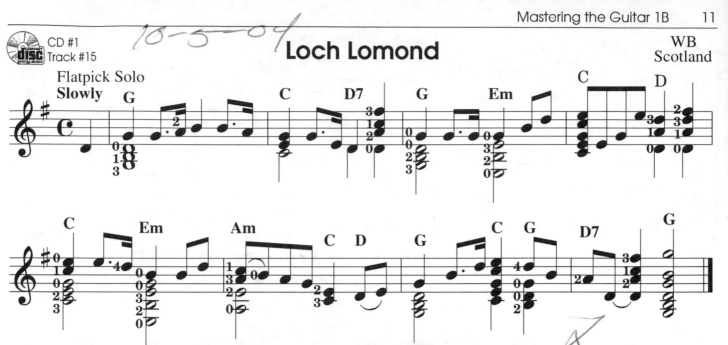

A New Chord: Bm

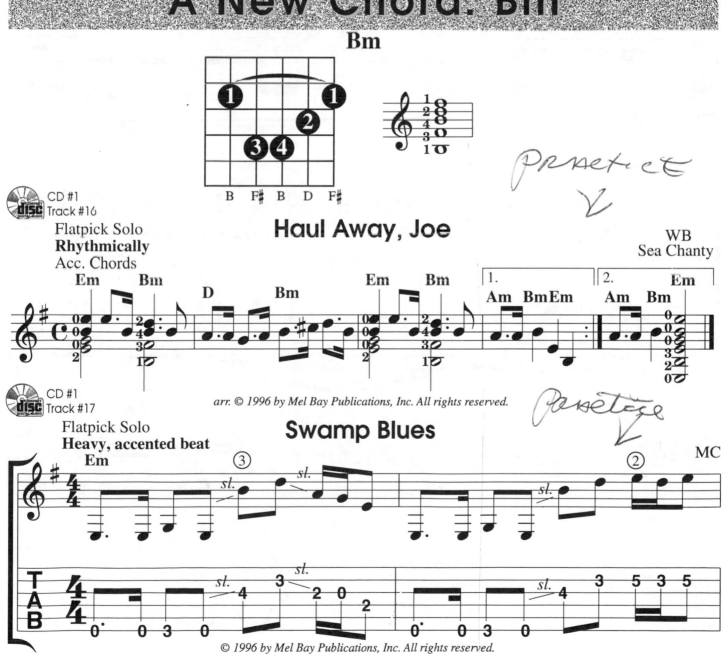

PRACTICE

CD #1
Track #16

Haul Away, Joe

WB
Sea Chanty

Flatpick Solo
Rhythmically
Acc. Chords

CD #1
Track #17

Swamp Blues

Flatpick Solo
Heavy, accented beat

MC

Swamp Blues con't

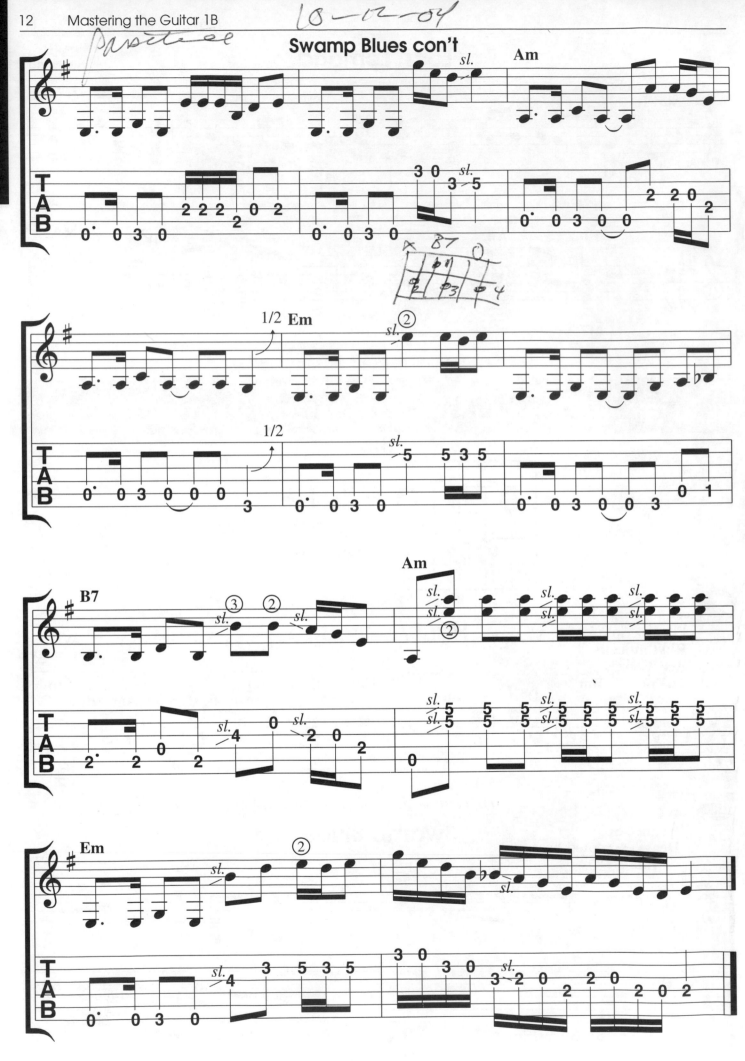

Study #1

Study #2

The Burning of the Piper's Hut

CD #1
Track #18

Flatpick Solo
Rhythmic
Acc. Chords

WB
Scottish March

16th Notes

16th Notes

10-26-04

Study #1

Study #2

CD #1
Track #19

Tango for Edgar

Flatpick Solo
Moderately

MC

Key of D

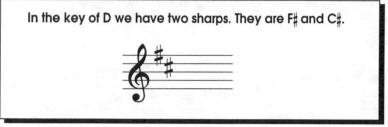

In the key of D we have two sharps. They are F# and C#.

PRACTICE IN 1ST & 2ND POSITION

11—0—04

D Scale

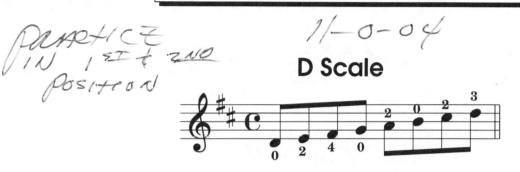

Velocity Study #1

WB

Velocity Study #2

WB

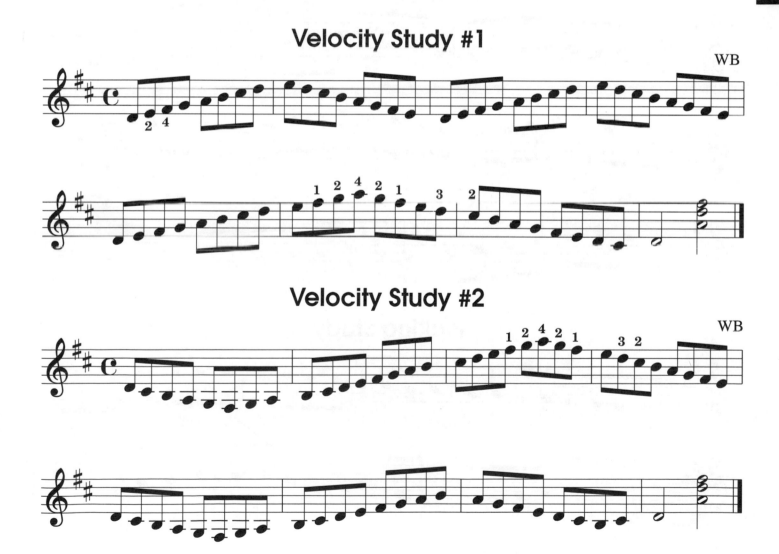

Key of D

11-2-04

Velocity Study #3

Velocity Study #4

Picking Study

Largo

(Play Fingerstyle)

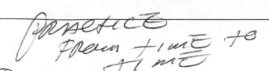

CD #1
Track #20

MC
Vivaldi

Fingerstyle Solo
Slowly

Key of D

└ Strum with the thumb.

D.C. al Coda

When you see the marking **D.C. al Coda,** go back to the beginning and play until you see the coda sign (⊕). When you reach the coda sign, skip down to the second coda sign or the ending.

CD #1
Track #21

Texas Tea

Flatpick Solo
Smoothly, connected

MC

To Coda ⊕

D.C. al Coda ⊕

CD #1
Track #22

Young McGoldrick

Flatpick Solo
Moderate tempo

WB

D.S. ℅ al Fine

CD #1
Track #23

Take One

Flatpick Solo
Fast

MC

CD #1
Track #24

Petronella

Flatpick Solo
Lively tempo
Acc. Chords

WB
Country Dance

Key of D

You and Me

Gavotte in D

George Frederic Handel

English Cradle Song

CD #1 Track #29

WB
English Carol

On this form of the G chord, do not play the 5th string. Deaden it by letting the fleshy part of your third finger touch the 5th string.

Cut Time

(Alla Breve)

The sign for cut time is 𝄵. This means to count each measure in ¹/₂ the time. Thus:

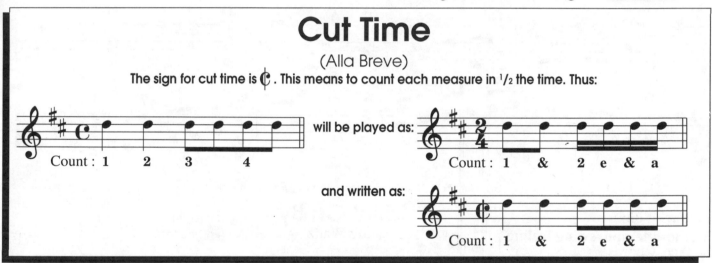

will be played as:

and written as:

Eighth of January

CD #1 Track #30

WB
Fiddle Tune

Key of D

Cuckoo's Nest

CD #1 Track #31

WB
Fiddle Tune

Flatpick Solo
Lively, dance tempo

Flatpick Solo
Slowly
Acc. Chords

Ode for Guitar

CD #1 Track #32

WB

Flatpick Solo
Fast
Acc. Chords

Bluegrass Break

CD #1 Track #33

WB

Key of D

CD #1
Track #34

Canon in D

MC
Pachelbel

Flatpick Solo
Moderately slow, flowing

Key of D

*Bar six strings in the second fret.

Key of D

CD #1
Track #35

Dance

WB
John Dowland

CD #1
Track #36

Dance from the Spanish Renaissance

WB
Gaspar Sanz

Key of D

CD #1
Track #37

English Carol
(O Little Town of Bethlehem)

WB

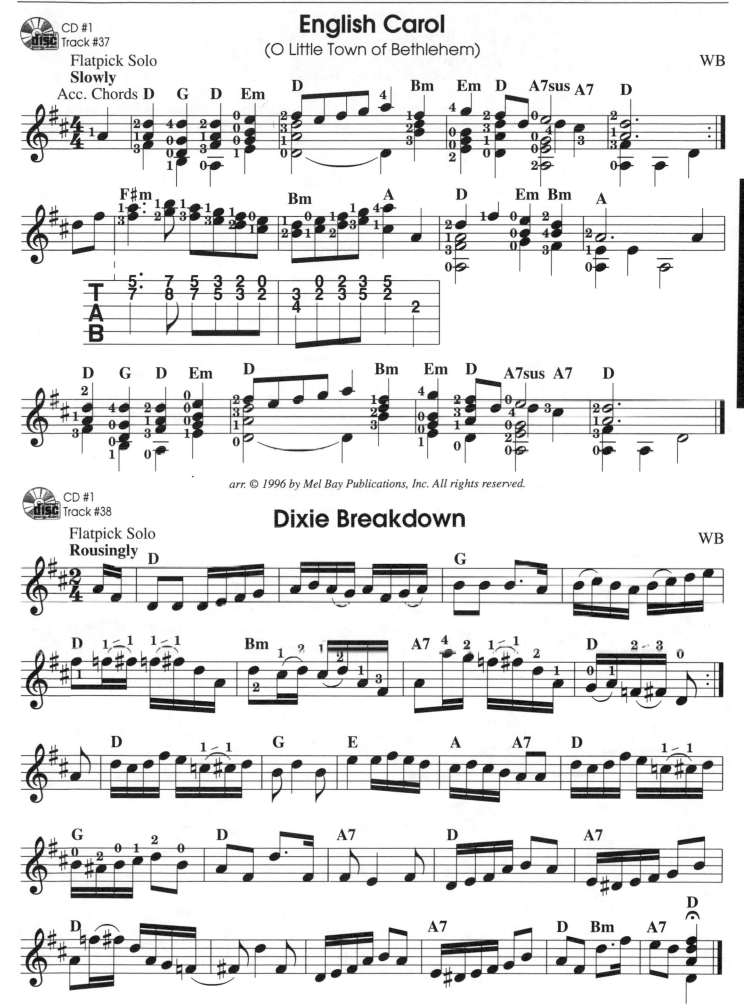

CD #1
Track #38

Dixie Breakdown

WB

Key of D

Dropped-D Tuning

When playing in the **key of D,** many beautiful voicings can be obtained by tuning the sixth string down to low D. To do this, play your fourth string; next play your sixth string and tune it down in pitch. It will be tuned to low D when it sounds one octave lower than your 4th string. In other words – keep lowering the note until, when compared to the open 4th string, no dissonance can be heard.

Here is what Low D looks like:

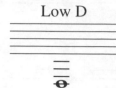

 CD #1
Track #39

Durin's Bane

(Tune 6th string down to Low D)

Remember – other notes on the sixth string will now be fingered two frets higher. Check out the tab on sixth string notes.

Dropped-D Tuning

Fingerstyle or Flatpick Solo   WB

⑥ = D **Freely, no strict tempo**

Key of D

Andante

CD #1
Track #40

Dropped-D Tuning
Flatpick Solo
Slowly

WB
Renaissance Lute Solo

Key of D

Fingerpicking Solos

I Saw Three Ships

Dropped-D Tuning
Fingerstyle Solo
Moderately, two beat feel

CD #1
Track #41

Trad. English
Carol
MC

Kemp's Jig

Dropped-D Tuning
Fingerstyle Solo
Bright

CD #1
Track #42

Anonymous
MC

Dropped-D Tuning
Fingerstyle Solo
Slowly & Gently
Acc. Chords

Paper of Pins

CD #1
Track #43

WB
American Ballad

Dropped-D Tuning
Fingerstyle Solo
No Set Tempo, Freely
Very slowly

The Galway Shawl

CD #1
Track #44

WB
Irish Ballad

Key of D

Gymnopedie

CD #1
Track #45

Dropped-D Tuning
Flatpick Solo
Slowly, gently

MC
E. Satie

Because of dropped D tuning,
play this G note sixth string, fifth fret

Key of D

CD #1
Track #46

Song

Play with the pick and then try it fingerstyle.

Flatpick or Fingerstyle Solo
Moderately

Carcassi

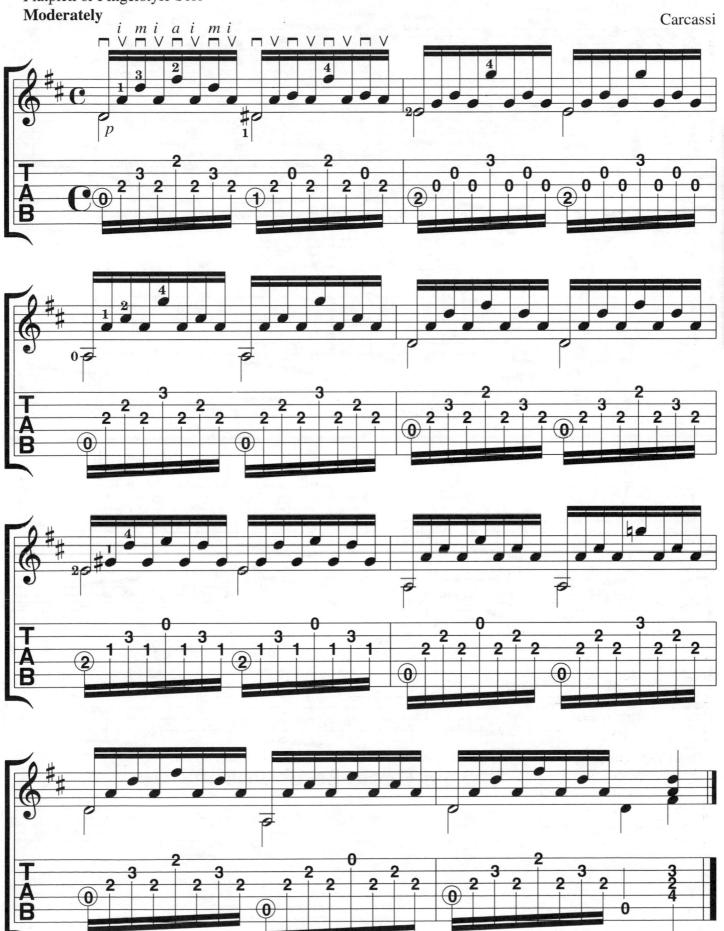

Key of D

The Shearing's Not For You

Dropped-D Tuning
Fingerstyle Solo
Acc. Chords

CD #1
Track #47

WB
Scotland

Dropped-D Tuning
⑥ = D   Fingerstyle Solo
Medium tempo
Acc. Chords

Will the Circle Be Unbroken?

CD #1
Track #48

WB
Gospel Song

Manhattan Nocturne

Dropped-D Tuning
Fingerstyle Solo
Slowly with feeling
Acc. Chords

CD #1
Track #49

WB

Chords in the Key of D

The chords in the key of D are written below:

D	Em	F#m	G	A	Bm
I	ii	iii	IV	V	vi

The new chords in this key are **F#m** and **A.** These chords are drawn below. There are two fingerings for the F#m. The fingering on the left is easier and requires the first finger to bar (lay) across three strings. The F#m on the right is a **barre chord.** It is called this because the first finger bars across all six strings. Strive to keep the first finger straight and next to the fret wire. Try not to let the strings pass under the knuckles. Rather than push with the flat part of the first finger, the finger is actually tilted slightly. Notice with the F#m the first finger is placed on the second fret. Also, notice the addition of the B minor barre chord. This Bm will sound more full than the Bm shown previously. Practice these new chords.

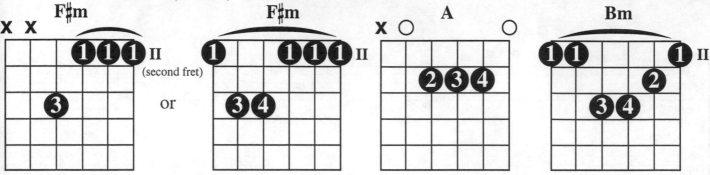

Practice the following exercises using chords from the **key of D.** Use strum or fingerpick patterns of your choice.

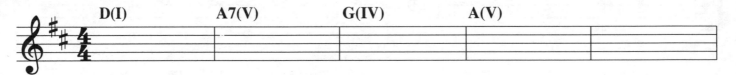

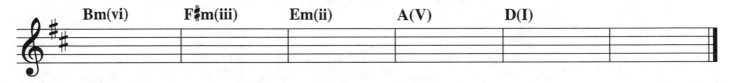

Practice strumming the chords to the following song in the **key of D.**

Shenandoah

Anon

1. Oh, Shen-an-doah, I long to hear you, A - way,____ you roll-ing riv - er.____ Oh Shen - an - doah I long to hear you, A - way,____ we're bound a - way, 'Cross the wide Mis - sou - ri.

Travis Picking

One type of fingerpick pattern which is used for 4/4 is referred to as **"Travis Pick."** In this style of picking, the right-hand thumb plays on each beat in the measure and alternates between two strings. The style is named after Merle Travis who popularized the technique of alternating the thumb. The right-hand fingers play between the thumb strokes. Written below are some common Travis Pick patterns. The patterns on the top show the basic Travis Pick, and the patterns on the bottom are variations. Both will work for 4/4. As with the other fingerpick patterns, each pattern takes one measure to complete. Hold any 6-, 5-, or 4-string chord and practice these patterns.

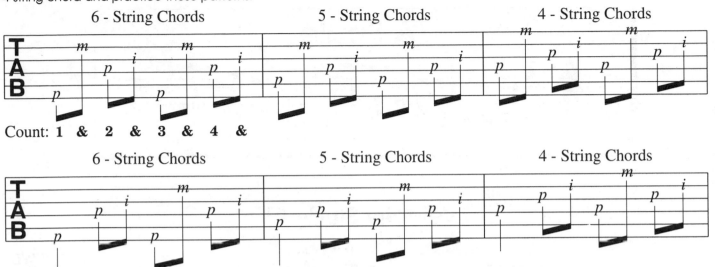

Practice the following song in the **key of D** using the Travis Pick for the accompaniment. To get started, the fingerpick is written under the first line. After using the basic Travis style, go back and play the song again using the variation of the Travis Pick. Remember, this style of fingerpicking can be used to play any song in 4/4 time.

Worried Man Blues

Traditional

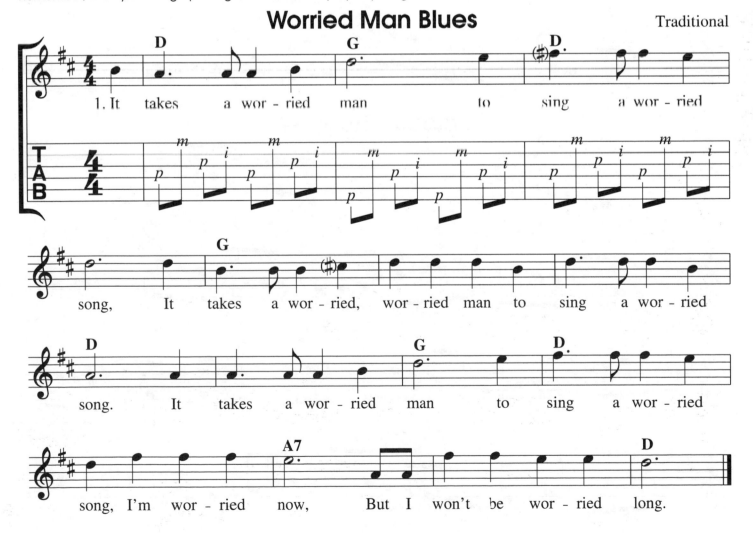

Key of A

In the key of A we have three sharps (F#, C#, G#). Here is the key signature from the key of A: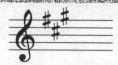

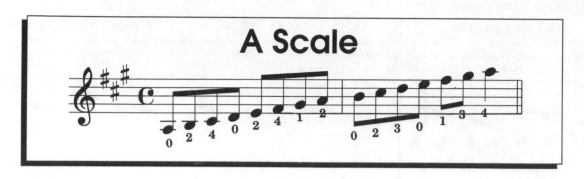

Velocity Study #1

Velocity Study #2

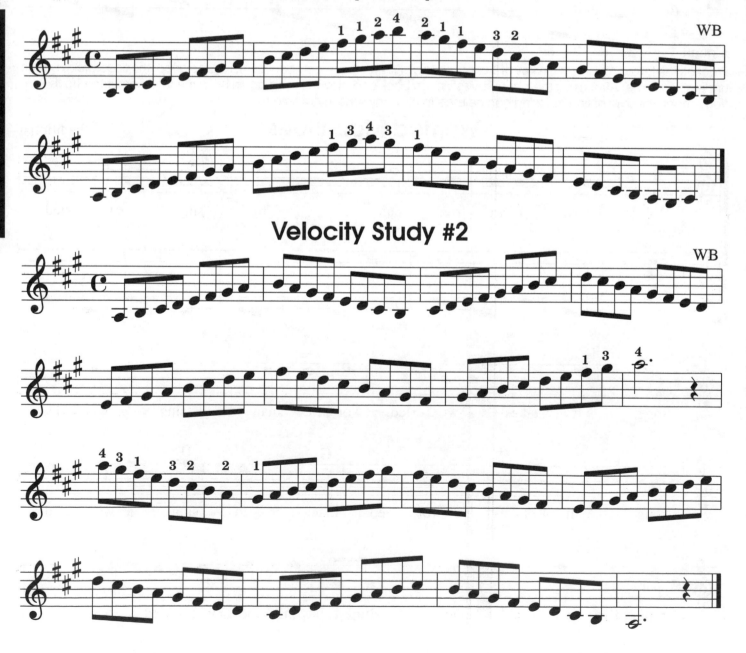

High C♯

High C♯

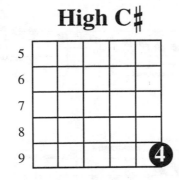

High C♯ is first string, ninth fret.

Velocity Study #3

WB

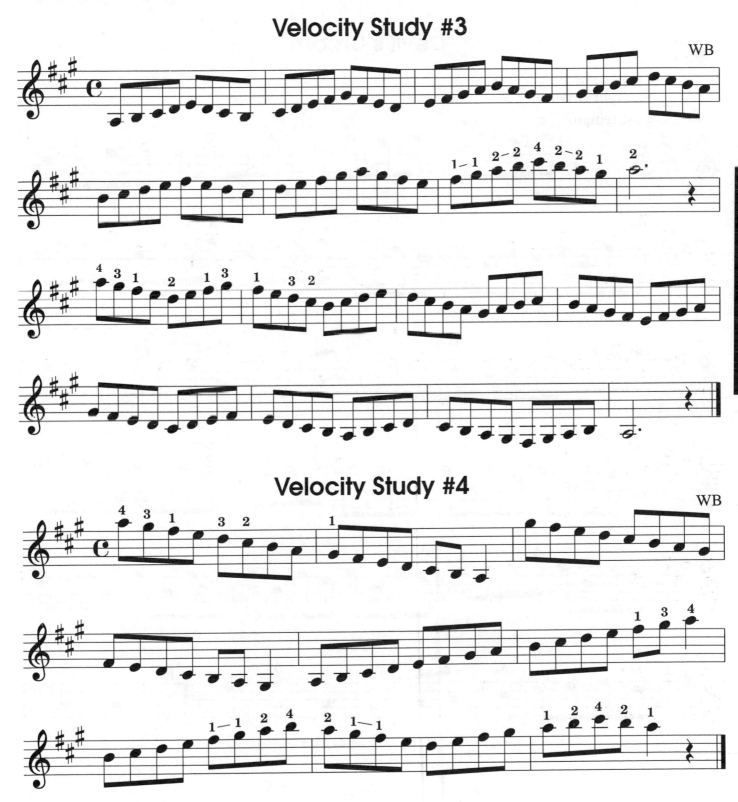

Key of A

Velocity Study #4

WB

Picking Study

Devil's Dream

CD #1
Track #50

Flatpick Solo
Straight rhythm
Fast tempo

MC
Fiddle Tune

WB

Harpswell

Flatpick Solo

WB

Allegro

Red Haired Boy

Flatpick Solo

WB
Fiddle Tune

Moderate tempo
Acc.Chords

Ballo Francese

WB
Don Giorgio Manierio

Flatpick Solo
Allegro
Acc. Chords

Il Est Né

WB
French Carol

Flatpick Solo
"March" Tempo
Acc. Chords

Key of A

Mere Point

CD #1
Track #55

Flatpick Solo
Bright tempo
Acc. Chords

WB

CD #1
Track #56

Dance

Flatpick Solo
Allegro
Acc. Chords

WB
Renaissance Lute Solo

Key of A

East Tennessee Blues

CD #1
Track #57

Flatpick Solo
Moderately
Swing feeling
Acc. Chords

WB
Fiddle Tune

CD #1
Track #58

I Feel Like Travelin' On

Flatpick Solo
Rhythmically

WB
Gospel Song

Volte

Flatpick Solo
Allegro
Acc. Chords

CD #1
Track #59

WB
Renaissance Lute Solo

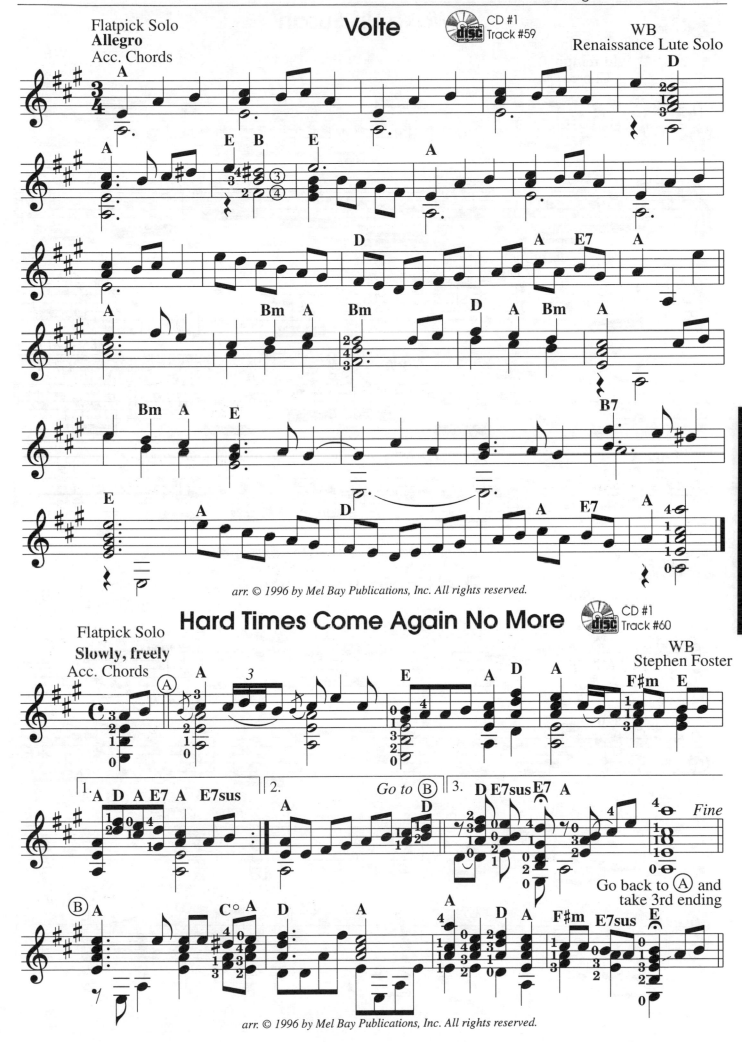

Hard Times Come Again No More

CD #1
Track #60

Flatpick Solo
Slowly, freely
Acc. Chords

WB
Stephen Foster

Go back to (A) and
take 3rd ending

Key of A

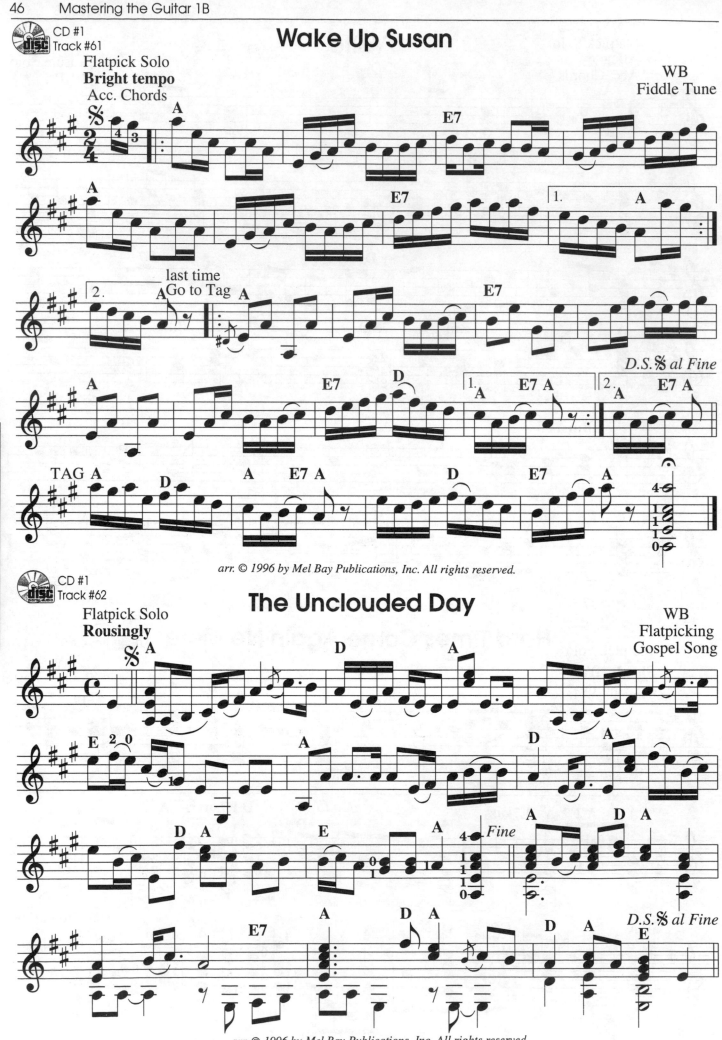

Key of A

Fingerpicking Solos

CD #1
Track #65

Estudio

Fingerstyle Solo
Moderately, smoothly

Diabelli

CD #1
Track #66

Walkin' Bass

Fingerstyle Solo
Easy feeling

WB

La Paloma

CD #1
Track #67

Fingerstyle Solo
Medium tempo

MC
Yradier

Key of A

Strum with the right-hand
index finger

Key of A

Simple Gifts

Fingerstyle Solo
Gently
Acc. Chords

CD #1
Track #68

WB
Shaker Song

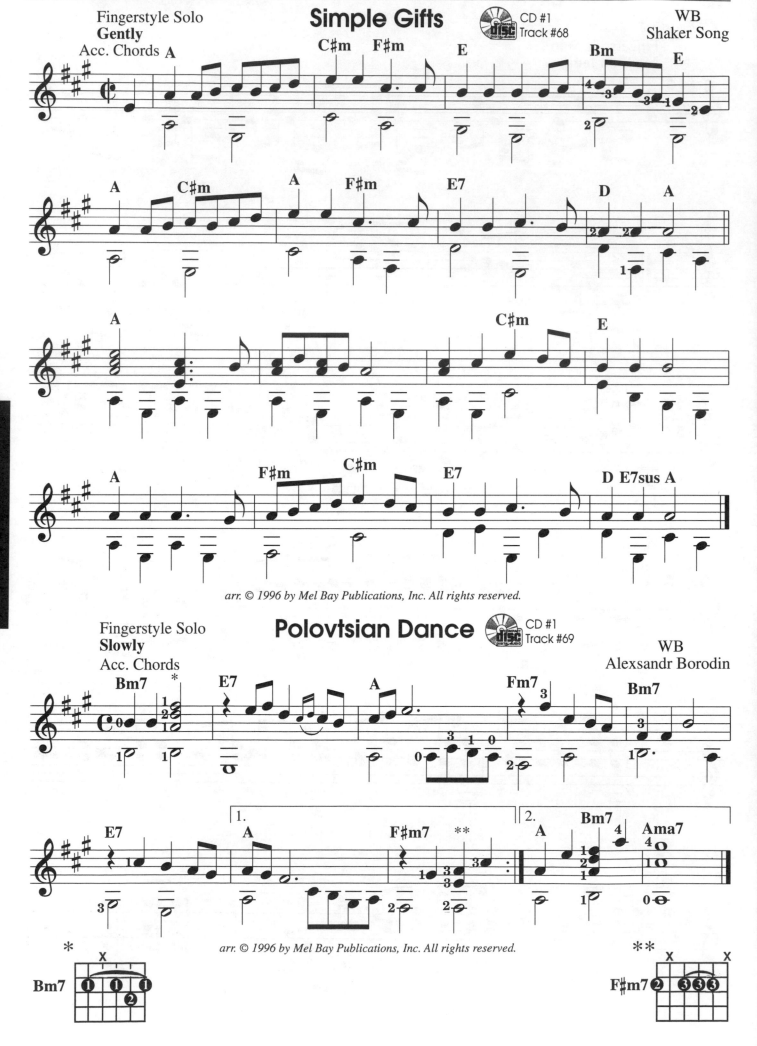

Polovtsian Dance

Fingerstyle Solo
Slowly
Acc. Chords

CD #1
Track #69

WB
Alexsandr Borodin

* Bm7

** F#m7

Darling Nelly Gray

CD #2
Track #1

Fingerstyle Solo
Slowly, freely

WB
Stephen Foster

Poem

CD #2
Track #2

Fingerstyle Solo
Slow ballad, with feeling

WB

Key of A

CD #2
Track #3

Jamaican Folksong

Anonymous
MC

Fingerstyle or Flatpick Solo
Moderate, easy feel

Key of A

* Bar 1/2 the strings (three strings) in the second fret.

Chords in the Key of A

Written below are the chords and their assigned Roman numerals for the **key of A.**

A	Bm	C♯m	D	E(7)	F♯m
I	ii	iii	IV	V	vi

The new chords in the key of A are: C♯m, and E. Two forms of the C♯m are drawn below. The one on the left is easier but the one on the right will sound more full. Also, the Bm barre chord is drawn below. This Bm will sound more full than the simple Bm used up until now. Notice the Bm is in the second fret, the C♯m chords are in the fourth fret. Also, notice the C♯m looks the same as Bm only two frets higher.

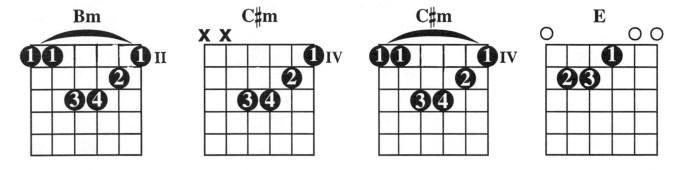

Practice playing the following exercises using chords in the **key of A.** Continue using the strum or fingerpick pattern suggested in the first measure, or use any of the strum or fingerpick patterns given earlier in this book.

Use all downstrokes on this exercise.

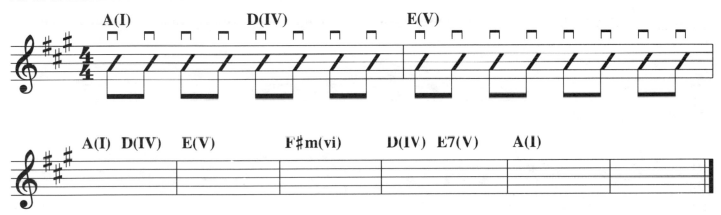

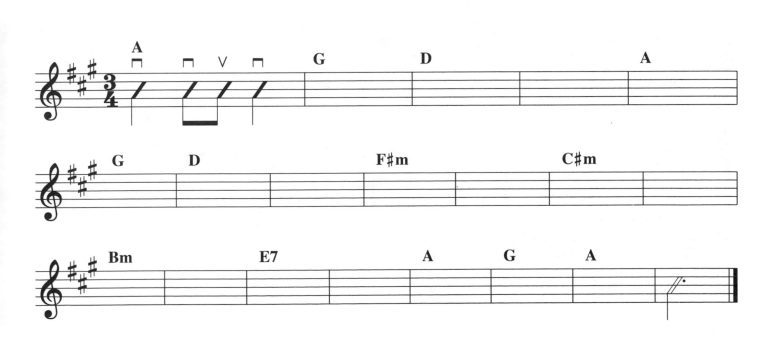

Chords in the Key of A

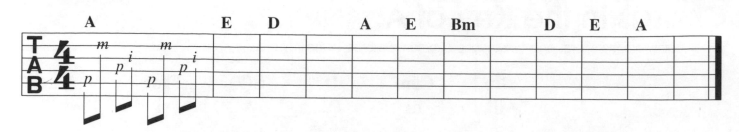

Practice the following song in the **key of A.** Travis pick or strum the chords. A sample of the Travis pattern has been written above the first measure.

Lonesome Road

Unknown

I'm   goin' down   that   long   lone – some   road,

I'm   goin' down   that   long – lone - some   road,

I'm   goin' down   that   long   lone-some   road,   Lord,   Lord,   and   I

ain't goin'   to   be   treat - ed   this   a   way.   Goin'   down   that

road   feel – ing   bad,   I'm   goin' down   that   road – feel - ing

bad,   Goin'   down   that   road – feel - in'   bad,   Lord,

Lord,   and   I   ain't goin'   to   be   treat - ed   this   a   way._____

Chord Symbols and Abbreviations

From here on in the book, chords other than major, minor, and seventh chords may be used.

The names of chords (symbols) can be written in several different ways. The chart below will help you know the symbols used for the different chord names. On the left is written the type of chord. On the right are the various symbols used in writing the chord names.

Major	major chords can be written with only the alphabet name (i.e. D, G, E, etc.). Major chords can also be sharp or flat (i.e. B♭, E♭, F♯, etc.). Major chords can also be written as Maj. or with a capital M next to the letter name of the chord.
Minor	m, -
Augmented	aug,+
Diminished	Dim, ○
Half Diminished	∅
Suspended	sus, sus4
Sixth	6
Minor Sixth	m6, -6
Seventh	7
Major Seventh	maj7, M7, 7̵, ma7, △, △7
Minor Seventh	m7, -7
Minor Major Seventh	m+7, m7̵
Seventh Suspended	7sus
Augmented Seventh	+7, 7+
Ninth	9
Major Ninth	maj9, M9, 9̵
Minor Ninth	m9, -9
Add Nine	add9, /9
Major Six Nine	6/9
Eleventh	11
Thirteenth	13

In altered chords, flat intervals can be written with a flat sign (♭) or a dash (–) before the name of the interval. For example, D seven flat nine would be written D7-9, or D7♭9. Sharp intervals in a chord can be written with a sharp sign (♯) or a plus sign (+) before the name of the interval. For example, E seven sharp nine would be written E7♯9, or E7+9. C seven, sharp five, flat nine would be written: C7♯5♭9, or C7+5-9.

Additional Chords in the Key of C

Drawn below are some additional chords which are commonly used in the key of C. Learn these chords and practice the exercises using them.

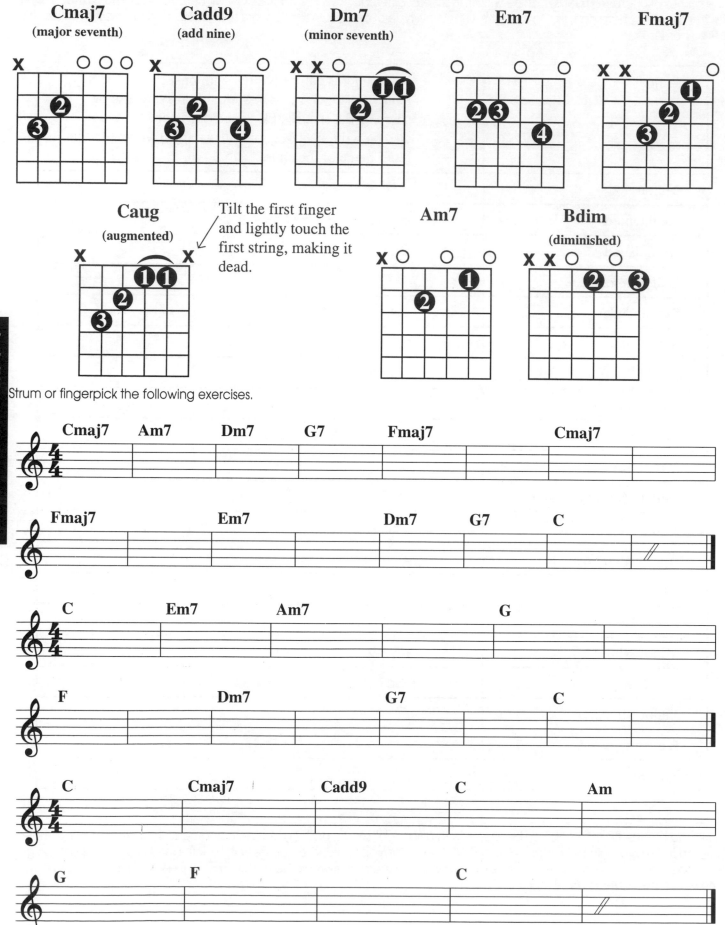

Tilt the first finger and lightly touch the first string, making it dead.

Strum or fingerpick the following exercises.

6/8 and 12/8 Strums

Written below are the strum patterns which work for songs in **6/8** and **12/8** time. Hold any chord and practice these patterns.

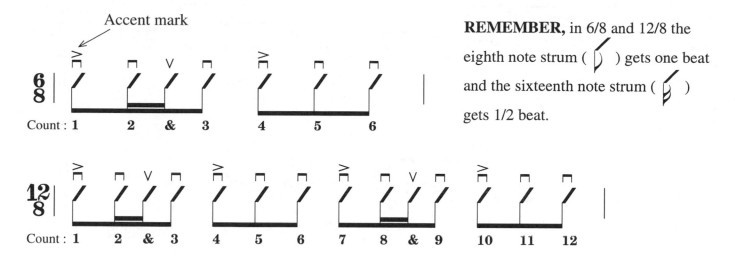

REMEMBER, in 6/8 and 12/8 the eighth note strum (♪) gets one beat and the sixteenth note strum (♬) gets 1/2 beat.

Practice the following progressions in **6/8** and **12/8.** Use the strum patterns which are written in the first measure to play each measure of the progression.

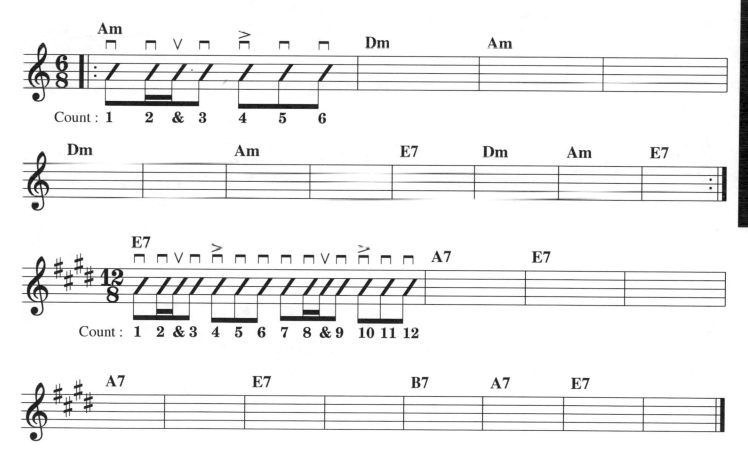

When Johnny Comes Marching Home

Traditional

When John-ny comes march-ing home a-gain, Hur-rah, Hur-

rah, When John-ny comes march-ing home a-gain, Hur-

rah, Hur-rah, The men will cheer and the

boys will shout, the la-dies they will all turn out and we'll

all be glad when John-ny comes march-ing home.

Practice the following song using the strum pattern for **12/8** time.

Goin' To See My Baby

6/8, 12/8 time

Key of E

The key of E has four sharps. They are F#, C#, G#, D#. Here is the key signature for the key of E:

D# Review

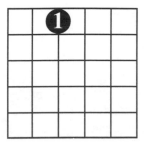

4th string, 1st fret

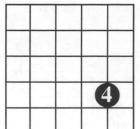

2nd string, 4th fret

Key of E Scale

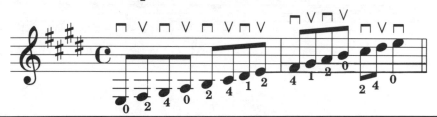

Velocity Study #1

WB

Velocity Study #2

WB

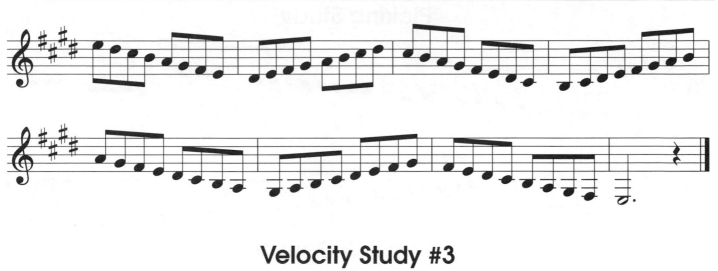

Velocity Study #3

Velocity Study #4

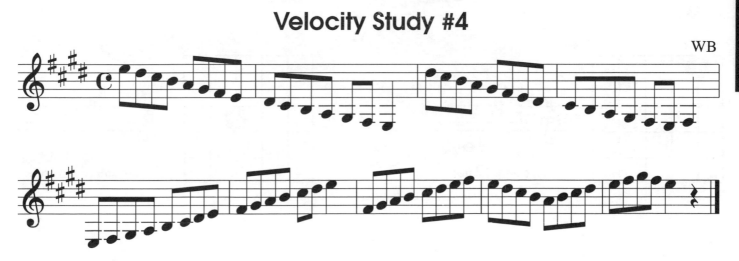

Key of E

Picking Study

WB

Brunswick Dance

CD #2
Track #4

Flatpick Solo
Lively tempo

WB

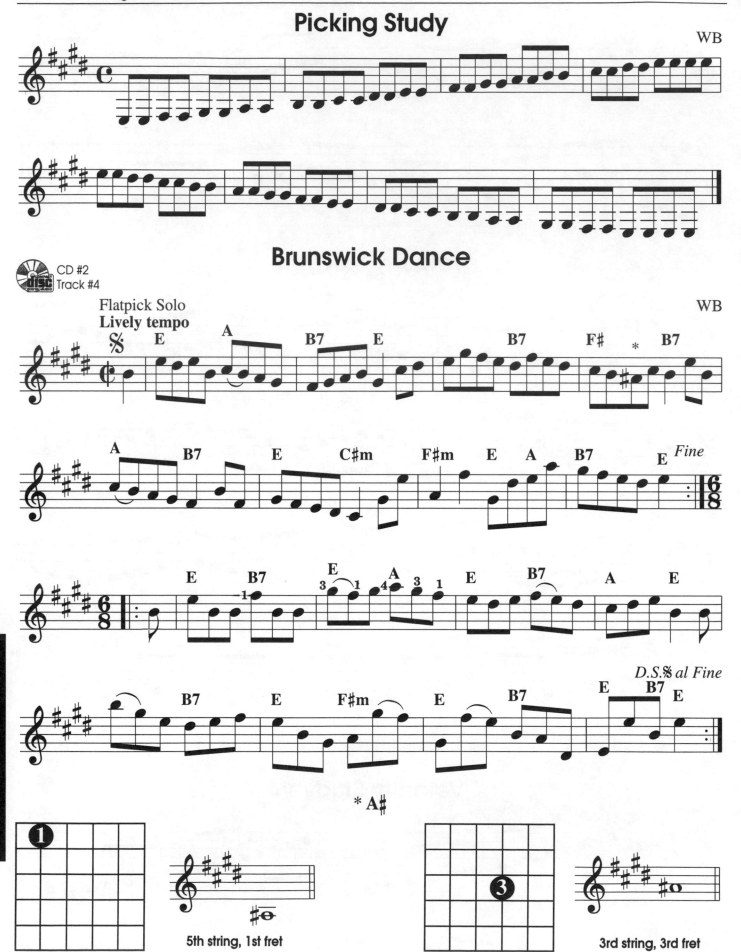

*A#

5th string, 1st fret

3rd string, 3rd fret

Key of E

CD #2
Track #5

Gateway Blues

Flatpick Solo
Driving rhythm

MC

Key of E

Collin's Quest

Flatpick Solo
Bright

WB

McKenna's Cove

Flatpick Solo
Medium tempo

WB

Key of E

Carolan's Draught

WB
O'Carolan

CD #2
Track #8

Flatpick Solo
Brisk

Ding Dong Merrily on High

WB
English Carol

CD #2
Track #9

Fingerstyle or Flatpick Solo
Brightly

Key of E

Upper Notes on the First String

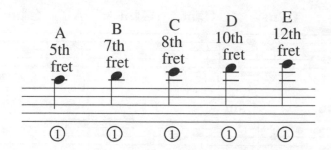

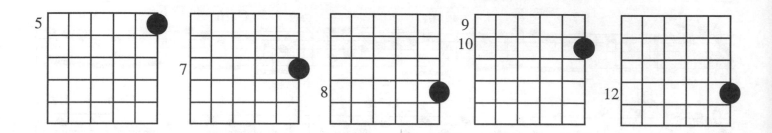

Play the following song in which *all of the notes are played on the first string*.

Malaga

CD #2
Track #10

Flatpick Solo
Gently

MC

Prairie Sunset

Flatpick Solo
Medium tempo

CD #2
Track #11
WB

Fingerstyle or Flatpick Solo
Slow blues

Been There – Done That

CD #2
Track #12
WB

Key of E

CD #2
Track #13

Recuerdo de Escorial

MC

Fingerstyle or Flatpick Solo
Moderately bright

Key of E

indicates up stroke

Key of E

CD #2
Track #14

Wilson's Hornpipe

WB
Fiddle Tune

Flatpick Solo
Moderate two feeling

Blues For Eric

CD #2
Track #15

MC

Flatpick Solo
Medium blues feet

Key of E

The Girl with the Flaxen Hair

MC
C. Debussy

Key of E

Fingerpicking Solos

Fingerstyle Solo
Walking tempo

Blues No. 79

CD #2
Track #17

MC

Fingerstyle Solo
Steady blues feel

Dusty's Blues

CD #2
Track #18

MC

Key of E

Battle Cry of Freedom

CD #2
Track #19

Fingerstyle Solo
Slowly, with feeling

WB
Civil War Song

CD #2
Track #20

Irish Hymn

Fingerstyle Solo
Flowing

WB
Gaelic Melody

Key of E

CD #2
Track #21

Lorena

WB
American Ballad

Fingerstyle Solo
Very slowly

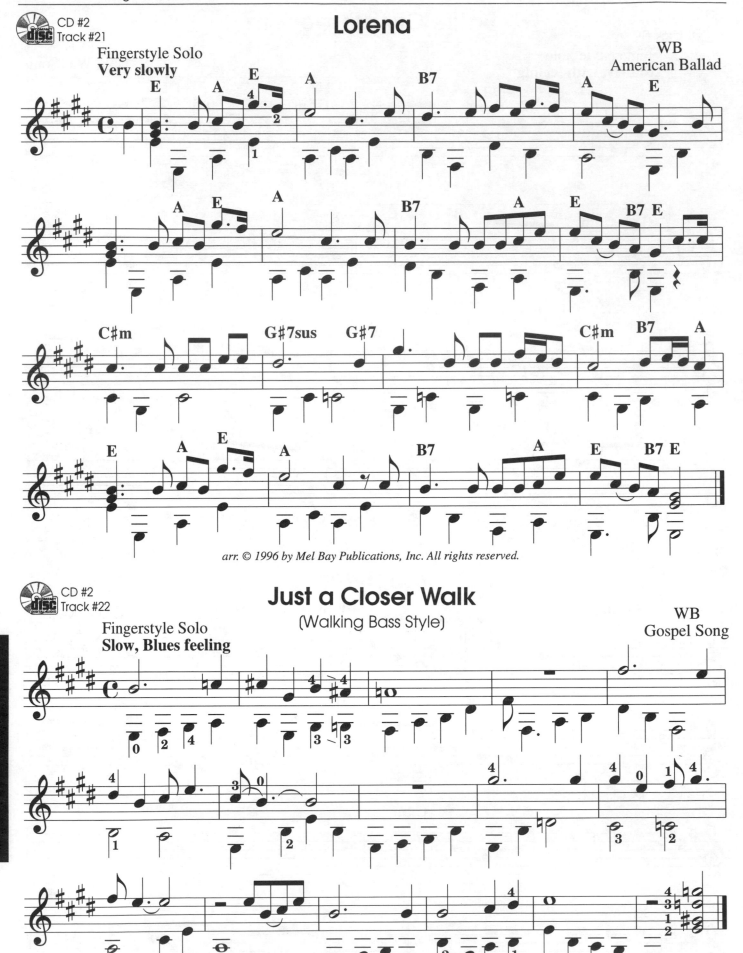

CD #2
Track #22

Just a Closer Walk
(Walking Bass Style)

WB
Gospel Song

Fingerstyle Solo
Slow, Blues feeling

Key of E

Etude

CD #2
Track #23

(Play with pick or fingers)

Fingerstyle or Flatpick Solo

Carulli

Moderately

Chords in the Key of E

The chords in the **key of E** are written below. The new chord in this key is **G#m,** which is a barre chord in the fourth fret.

E	F#m	G#m	A	B7	C#m
I	ii	iii	IV	V	vi

G#m

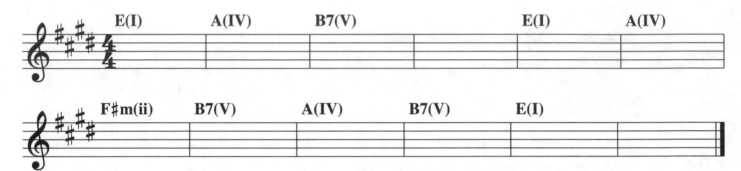

Practice fingerpicking or strumming the following exercises in the **key of E.**

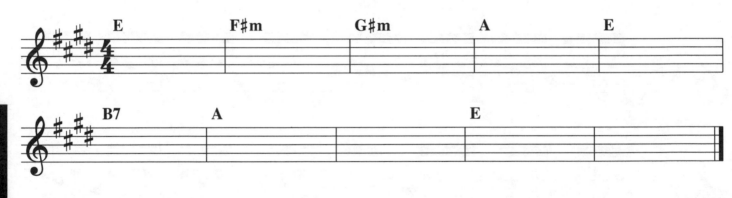

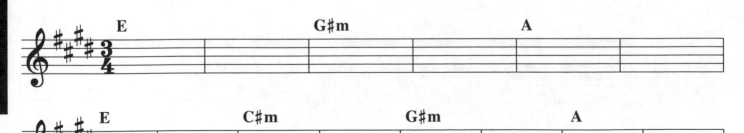

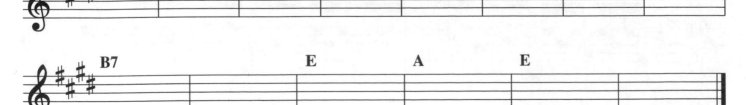

Fingerpicking 3/4 Time

A commonly used fingerpick pattern for **3/4** time is written on the tablature below. Hold any of the 6-, 5-, or 4-string chords and learn this pattern. This fingerpick pattern can be used to play any song in 3/4. Each pattern takes one measure to complete.

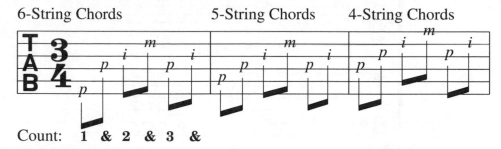

6-String Chords   5-String Chords   4-String Chords

Count: 1   &   2   &   3   &

This fingerpick can be played with even eighth notes, or with a swing rhythm in which each beat is divided into a long-short pattern. Practice the following exercise first with even eighth notes, and then swing the eighth notes.

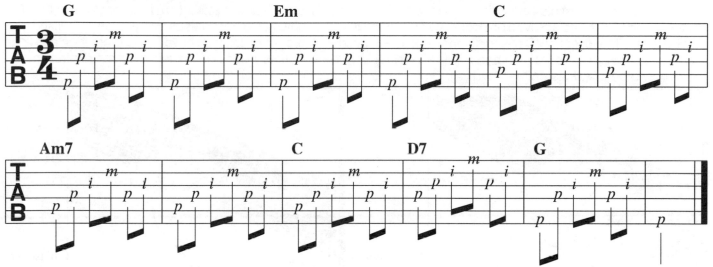

Play the following song in the **key of E** using the fingerpick pattern for 3/4. A sample of the pattern has been written above the first measure.

Amazing Grace

Traditional

A - maz - ing __ Grace, How sweet the sound that saved a __ wretch like _ me. _____ I __ once was _ lost, but now I am found, was blind but __ now I see. _____

The Bend

A *bend* is written with a curved arrow next to the note. If ¹/₂ is written by the arrow, bend the note so it sounds ¹/₂ step (one fret) higher than the written note. If "full" is written, bend the note so it sounds one whole step (two frets) higher than the written note. To play a bend, first play the written note and then bend the string. If the note is played on strings one or two, bend the string upward. If the note is played on strings five or six, bend the string downward. For notes on strings three or four, the string can be bent either direction. Depending on the gauge of strings you are using, you may have to use more than one finger on the same string to help with the bend. Illustration No. 1 shows how a bend is done on the second string. Illustration No. 2 shows how a bend is done on the fifth string.

Illustration No. 1

Illustration No. 2

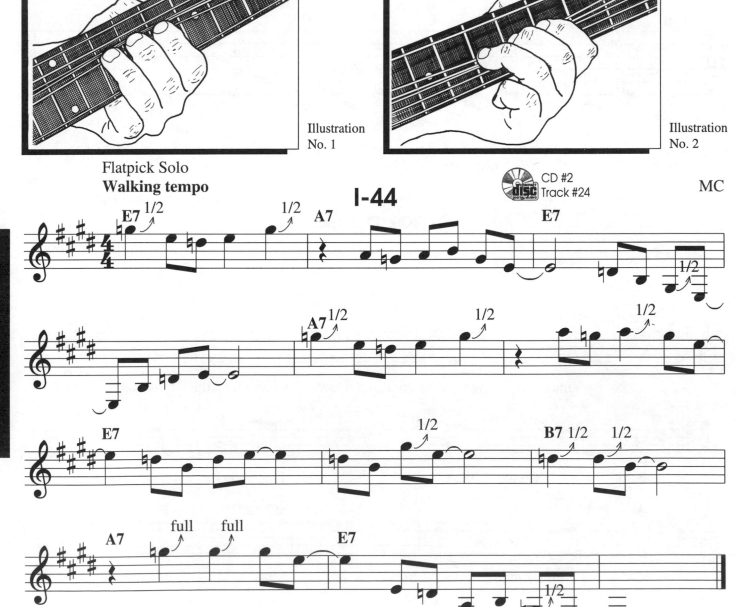

Flatpick Solo
Walking tempo

CD #2
Track #24

MC

I-44

The Bend

Corey's Blues

CD #2
Track #25

Flatpick Solo
Slow blues

MC

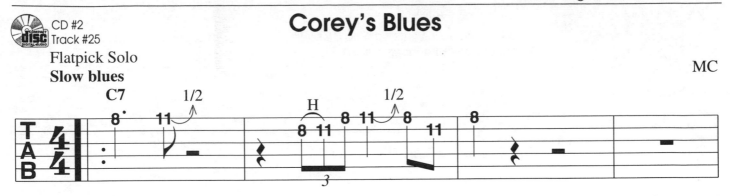

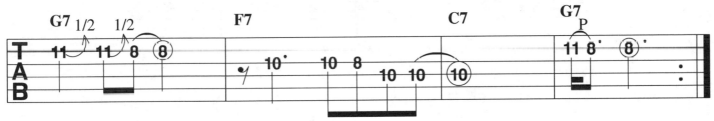

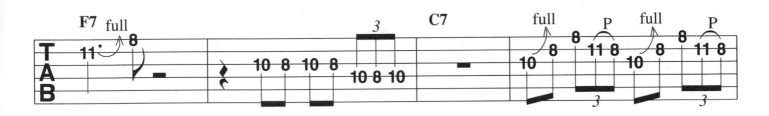

CD #2
Track #26

Birch Canyon Blues

Flatpick Solo
Moderate

MC

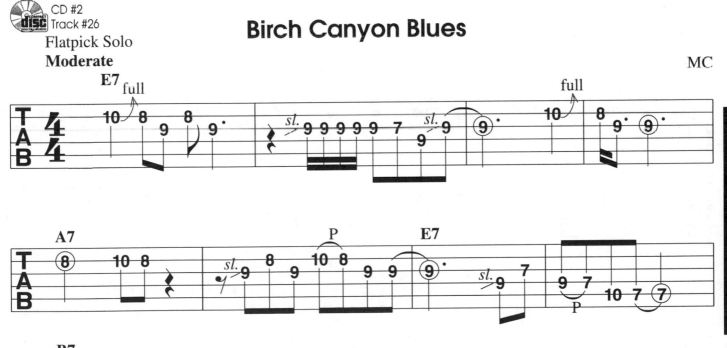

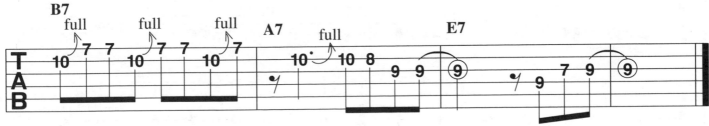

The Bend

Flats

A **flat** (♭) placed in front of a note *lowers* the pitch ½ step or one fret. Study the notes below. A **natural sign** (♮) cancels out a flat.

1st String

2nd String

3rd String

4th String

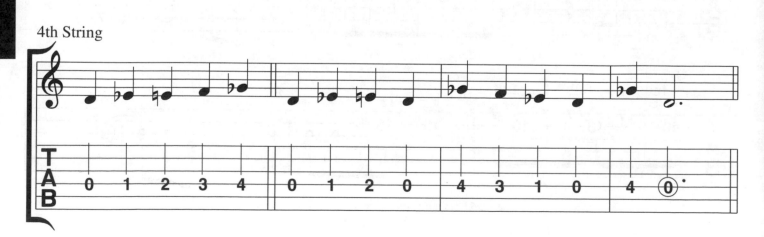

5th String

6th String

Benny's Flat

Flatpick Solo
Bright

WB

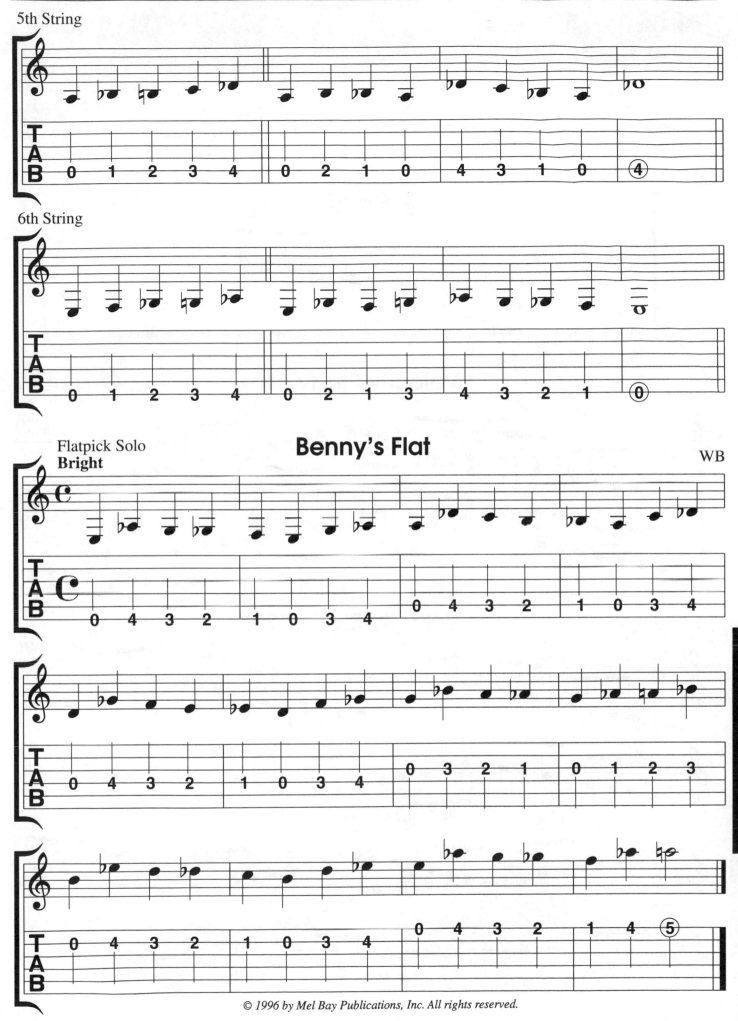

Flats

Key of F

In the key of F, we have one flat – B♭. Here is the key signature for the key of F:

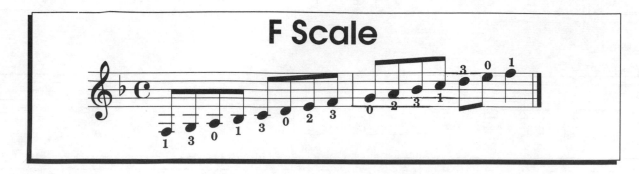

Velocity Study #1

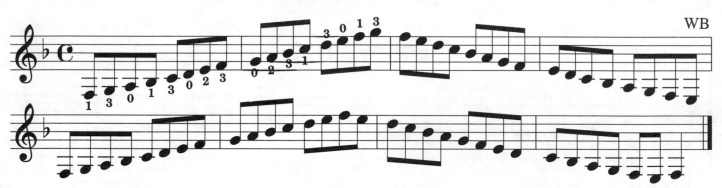

Velocity Study #2

Velocity Study #3

WB

Velocity Study #4

WB

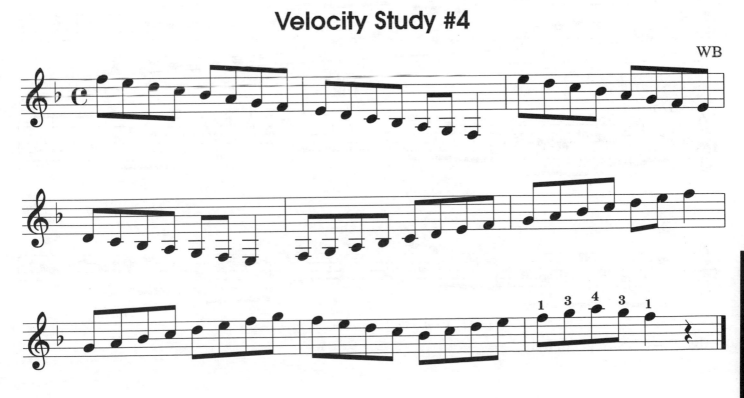

Key of F

F Picking Study

WB

CD #2
Track #27

Etude in F

Flatpick Solo
Moderately fast

WB

*High B♭—1st string, 6th fret.

Key of F

The Holly and the Ivy

CD #2
Track #28

MC

Flatpick Solo
Gently

Goin' Home

CD #2
Track #29

MC

Flatpick Solo
Medium, steady tempo

Key of F

Angels We Have Heard On High

Flatpick Solo
Moderately

CD #2
Track #30

WB
French Carol

Blackberry Blossom

Flatpick Solo
Lively

CD #2
Track #31

WB
Fiddle Tune

Celtic Twilight

Flatpick Solo
Freely, slow

CD #2
Track #32

WB

Key of F

Key of F

CD #2
Track #36

Penses

(Guitar Duet)

Fingerstyle or Flatpick
Slow, dream like

WB

Key of F

East Wind

CD #2
Track #37   MC

It Don't Matter To Me

CD #2
Track #38   MC

Key of F

Chords in the Key of F

The chords in the **key of F** with their assigned Roman numerals are written below. The new chords in the key of F are: Gm, Bb, and C7, These chords are drawn below in the key.

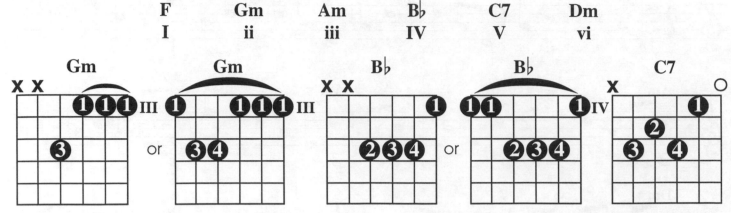

Practice the following progressions using chords in the **key of F.** You may want to use the simple Gm and Bb chords first and then use the barre chords. On the following exercises, if the accompaniment pattern is not suggested, use strum or fingerpick patterns presented earlier in this book.

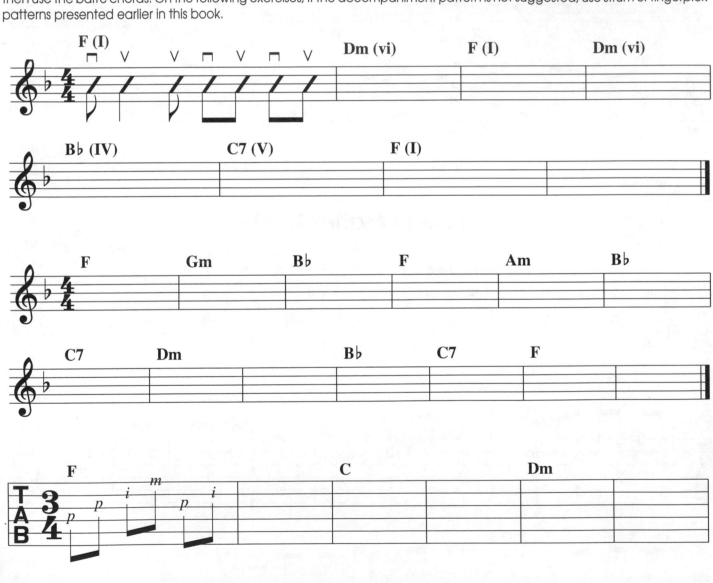

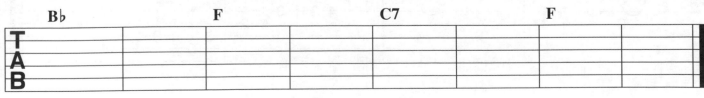

Practice playing the chords to the following song in the **key of F.** A suggested fingerpick pattern to use is written above the first measure.

The Water Is Wide

English
Folk Melody

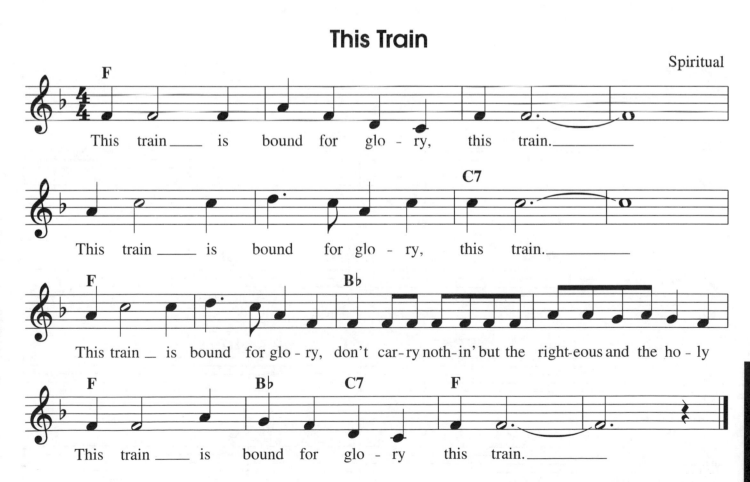

The wa-ter is wide, I can-not get o'er, _____ and neith - er have _____ I wings to fly, _____ give me a boat _____ that can car - ry two, _____ and both shall row, _____ my true love and I. _____

This Train

Spiritual

This train _____ is bound for glo - ry, this train. _____

This train _____ is bound for glo - ry, this train. _____

This train _ is bound for glo - ry, don't car-ry noth-in' but the right-eous and the ho - ly

This train _____ is bound for glo - ry this train. _____

Additional Chords in the Key of G

Drawn on the diagrams below are some additional new chords which are often used in the **key of G.** Learn the chords and practice the exercises.

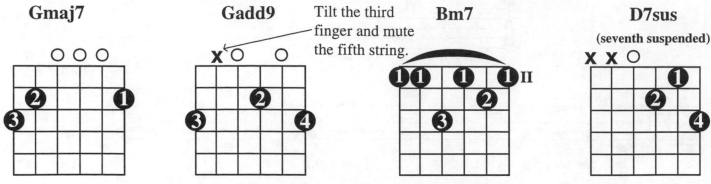

Gmaj7 **Gadd9** Tilt the third finger and mute the fifth string. **Bm7** **D7sus** (seventh suspended)

Use strum or fingerpick patterns to play the following exercises.

If you've forgotten this chord, look under "Additional Chords in the Key of C."

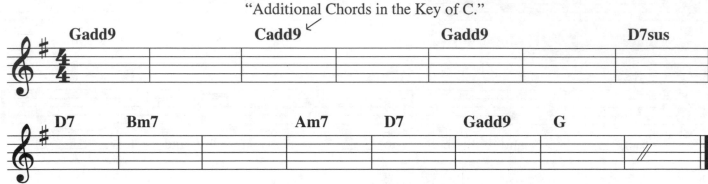

| Gadd9 | Cadd9 | Gadd9 | D7sus |

| D7 | Bm7 | Am7 | D7 | Gadd9 | G |

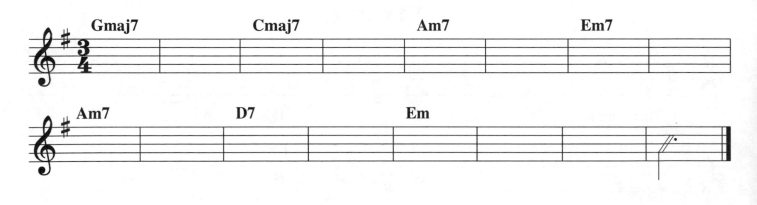

| Gmaj7 | Cmaj7 | Am7 | Em7 |

| Am7 | D7 | Em |

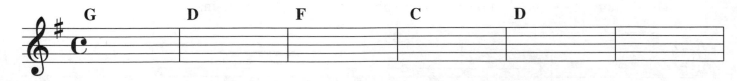

| G | D | F | C | D |

| Em7 | Cmaj7 | Em7 | G | D7sus |

| D7 | C | G |

Key of D Minor

In the key of D minor we have one flat - B♭. Thus, the key of D minor is "relative" to the key of F major.

High Note Review

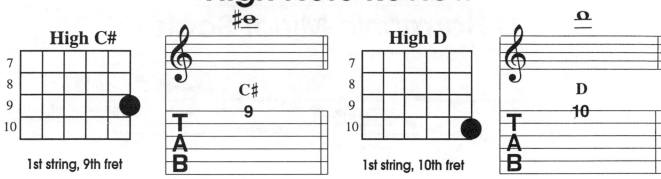

High C#

1st string, 9th fret

C#
9

High D

1st string, 10th fret

D
10

D Natural Minor Scale

Velocity Study #1

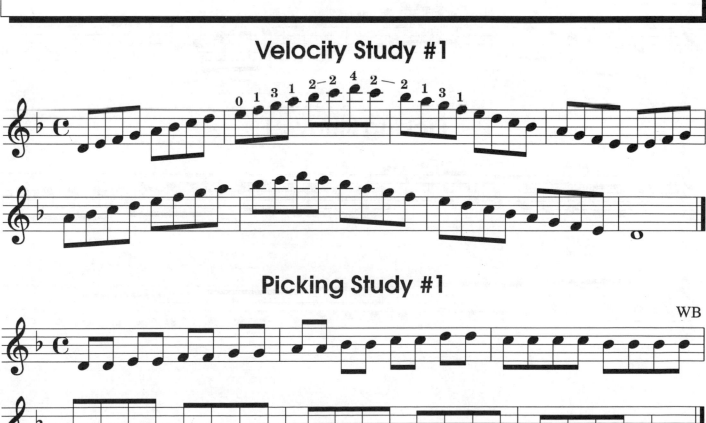

Picking Study #1

WB

D Harmonic Minor

In the D Harmonic Minor Scale, the 7th tone – C – is sharped.

D Harmonic Minor Scale

Velocity Study #1

WB

Picking Study #1

WB

$\frac{6}{4}$ Time

In 6/4, there are six beats in a measure, and the quarter note gets one beat.

Fandango

CD #2
Track #39
Flatpick Solo
Fast
Dm   MC

CD #2
Track #40

Lady's Fancy

Flatpick Solo
Rousingly

WB
Fiddle Tune

CD #2
Track #41

Sea of Glass

(Duet)

Flatpick or Fingerstyle
Slow, flowing tempo

Key of D minor

Key of D minor

Satan's Last Stand

Dropped-D Tuning
Flatpick or Fingerstyle
Slowly

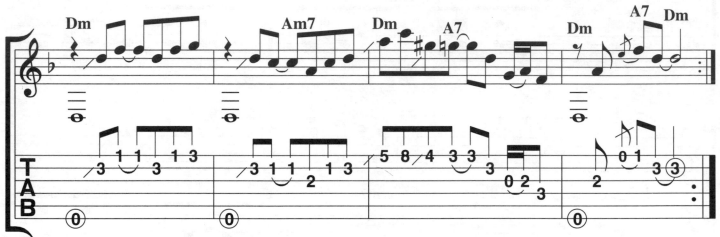

Brush Creek

Flatpick Solo
Bright

The Rights of Man

CD #2
Track #44

WB
Celtic Tune

Flatpick Solo

CD #2
Track #45

Jonah's Wake

Dropped-D Tuning

Flatpick or Fingerstyle Solo

WB

Key of D minor

CD #2
Track #46

Star in the Night

[Duet]

Guitar I - Flatpick
Guitar II - Fingerstyle
Flowing tempo - In 2

WB

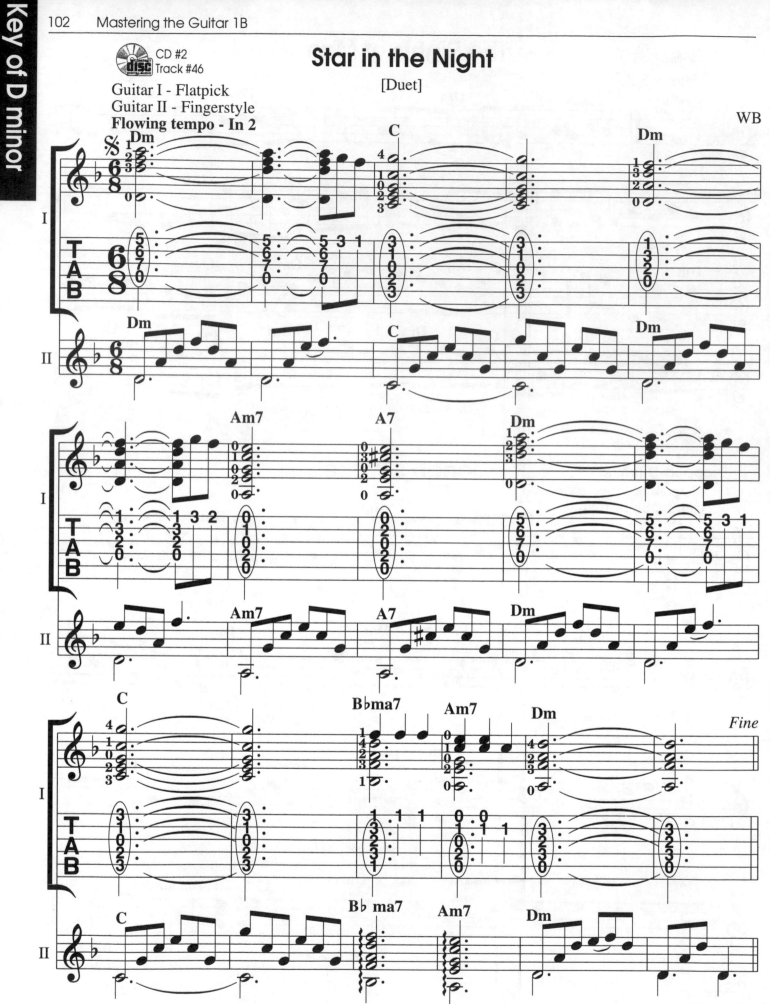

CD #2
Track #47

Welcome, Welcome Ev'ry Guest

Dropped-D Tuning
Flatpick Solo
Slowly

WB
Southern
Shaped Note Song

Song for Marcel

CD #2
Track #48

Key of D minor

Dropped-D Tuning

Flatpick Solo

Moderately

WB

Fingerstyle Solos

Fingerstyle Solo
Medium tempo, flowing

Españoleta

CD #2
Track #49

Gaspar Sanz

Fingerstyle Solo
Moderately

Long Time Gone

CD #2
Track #50

MC

Prayer

CD #2
Track #51

WB

Key of D minor

CD #2
Track #52

Seven Long Years

WB
Appalachian Song

Dropped-D Tuning

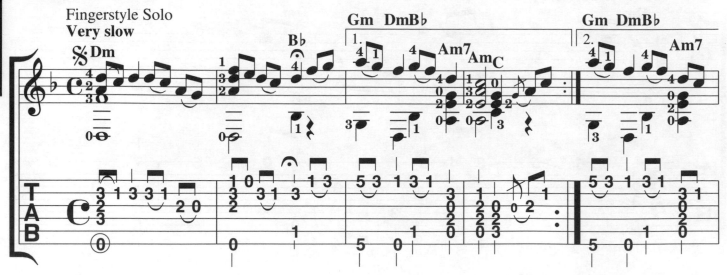

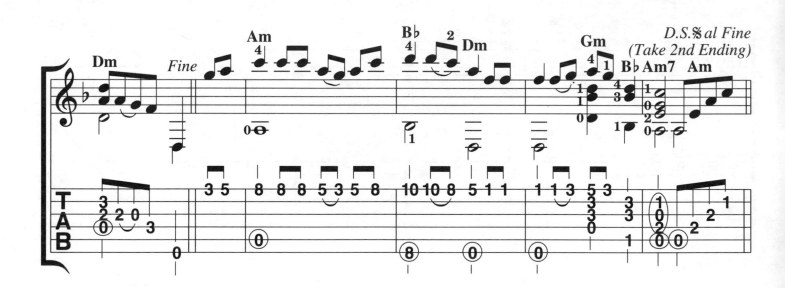

CD #2
Track #53

The Lonesome Dove

Key of D minor

Dropped-D Tuning

Fingerstyle Solo

WB
Appalachian Song

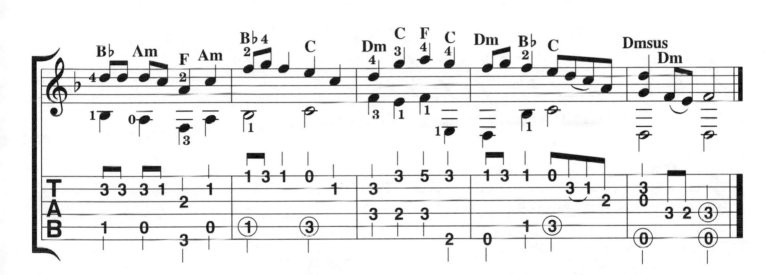

Chords in the Key of D Minor

Written below are the three primary chords in the **key of D minor.** Learn these chords and practice the following exercises and song in D minor. For the exercises, you can use the suggested strum or fingerpick written in the first measure, or use any of the other strum or fingerpick patterns.

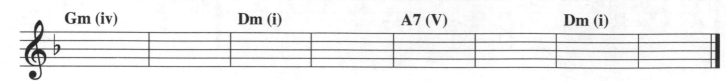

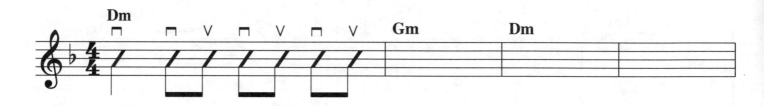

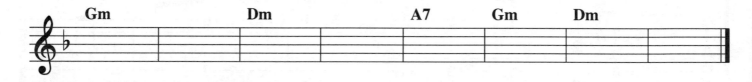

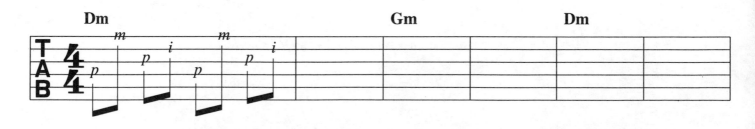

In the following song, the fingerpick accompaniment has been written beneath the melody. This will be helpful in learning the fingerpick and show how to fingerpick two chords in one measure (measure eight).

CD #2
Track #54

Scarborough Fair

Play the strings at the same time.

Play the strings together on the first beat, and let them ring through beats two and three.

arr. © 1996 by Mel Bay Publications, Inc. All rights reserved.

Chords in the Key of D minor

Key of B♭

In the key of B♭ major, we have two flats – B♭ and E♭.

Review

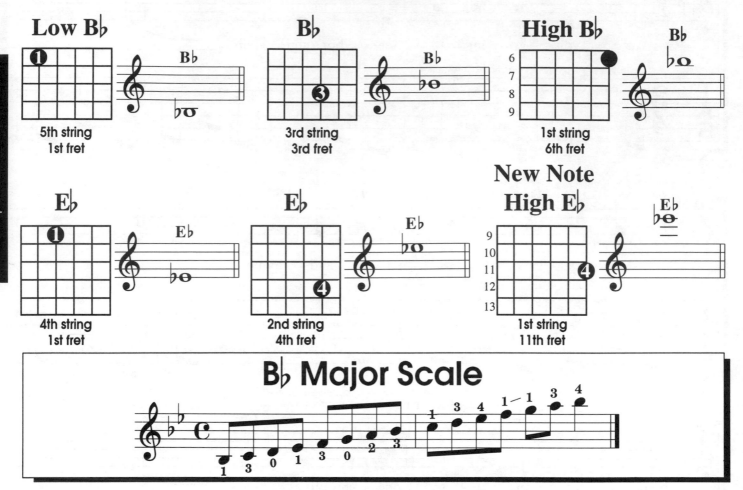

Low B♭
5th string
1st fret

B♭
3rd string
3rd fret

High B♭
1st string
6th fret

E♭
4th string
1st fret

E♭
2nd string
4th fret

New Note
High E♭
1st string
11th fret

B♭ Major Scale

B♭ Velocity Study #1

WB

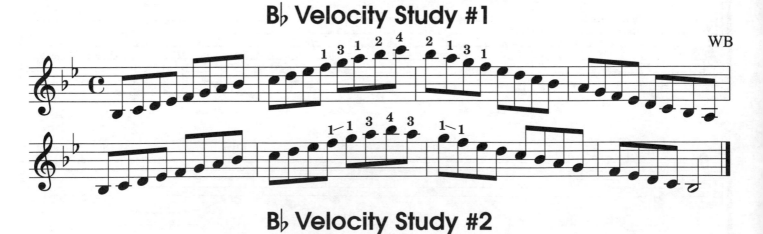

B♭ Velocity Study #2

WB

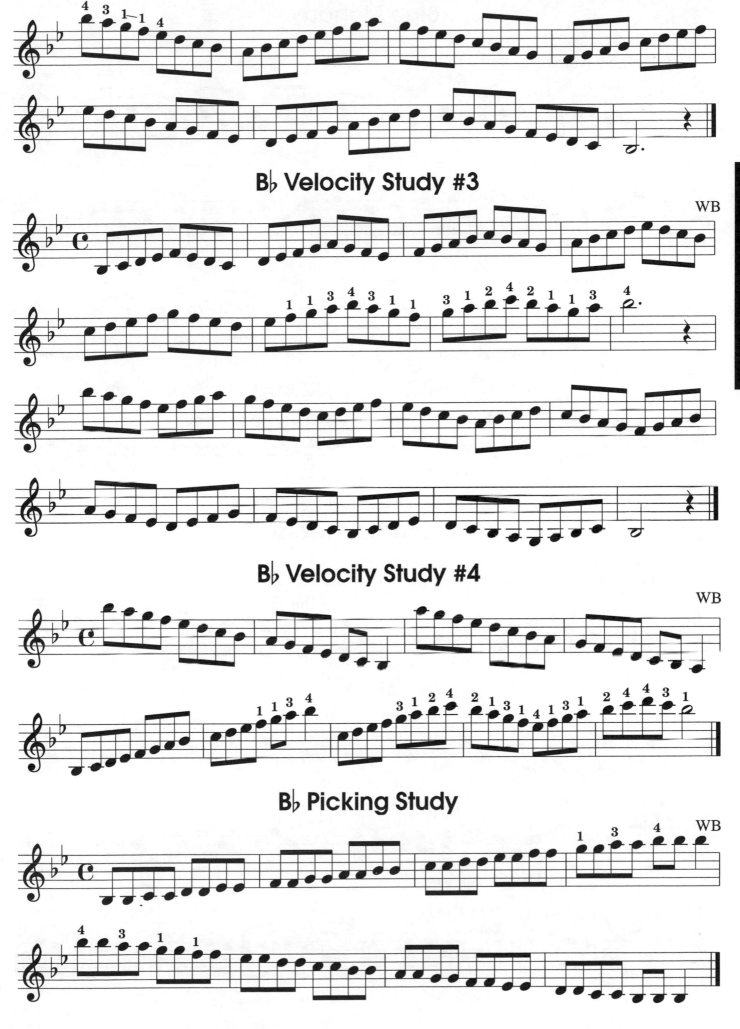

Bb Velocity Study #3

Bb Velocity Study #4

Bb Picking Study

Blue Monday

Flatpick Solo
Walking tempo

MC

Acoustic Dream

Flatpick Solo
Flowing (When possible, let the notes ring through the measure.)

MC

Key of Bb

CD #2
Track #57

Billy in the Lowground

Flatpick Solo
Allegro

WB
Fiddle Tune

CD #2
Track #58

Jezzy's Rag

Flatpick Solo
Moderately, two beat feel
Swing feeling

WB

CD #2
Track #59

Reverie

Flatpick Duet
Slowly

WB

Key of B♭

CD #2
Track #60

Cajun Cooker

A popular strumming style for pieces in 4/4 like "Cajun Cooker" is written below.

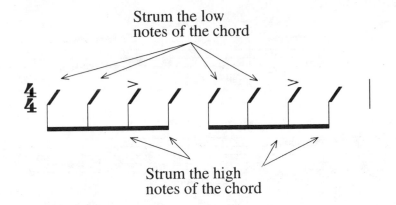

Strum the low
notes of the chord

Strum the high
notes of the chord

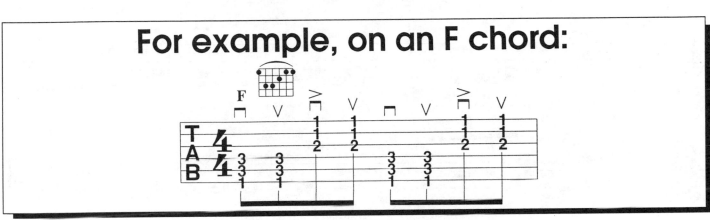

For example, on an F chord:

Flatpick Solo   MC
Fast

CD #2
Track #61

Funk Drive

WB

Flatpick Solo
Driving, medium tempo

CD #2
Track #62

Grand Slam

WB

Flatpick Solo
Laid - back feel

Thinking of Kathy

Fingerstyle Solo
Medium tempo
Bossa nova

CD #2
Track #63

MC

Key of B♭

Chords in the Key of B♭

The basic chords in the **key of B♭** are written below. The new chords in this key are **E♭**, **Cm**, and **F7**.

B♭	Cm	Dm	E♭	F(7)	Gm
I	ii	iii	IV	V	vi

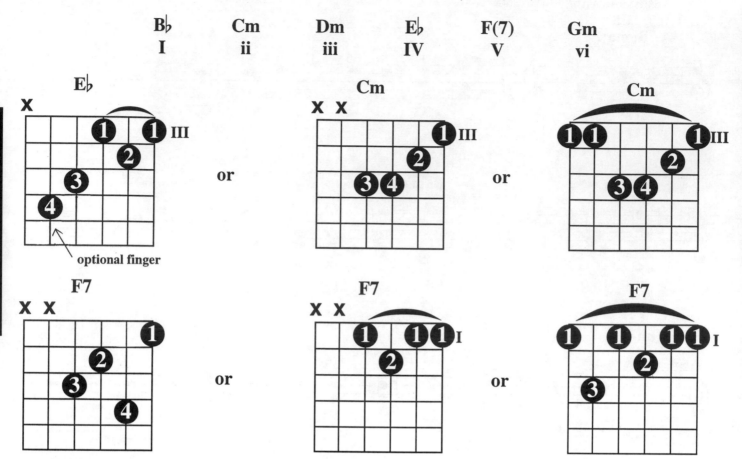

optional finger

or

or

Practice the following exercises using chords in the key of B♭. A suggested strum or fingerpick pattern to use has been written in the first measure.

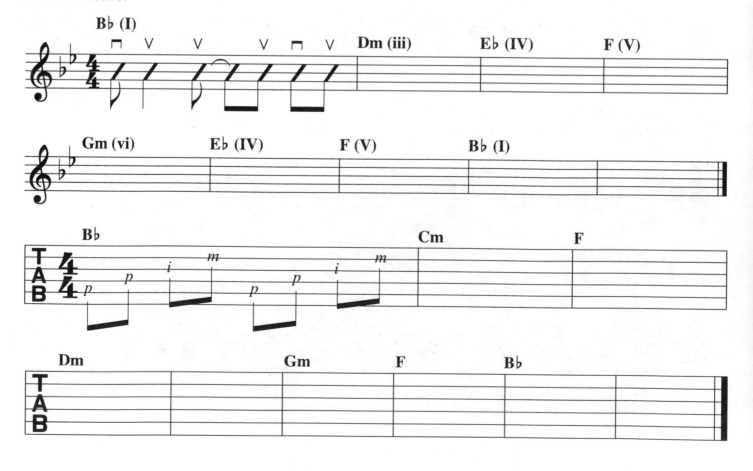

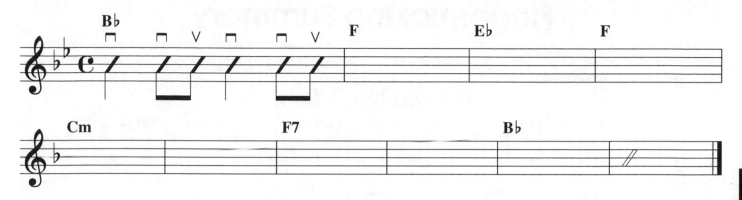

Play the chords to following song in B♭. The suggested strum pattern to use is written above the first measure.

Ain't No Cure

MC

I went to the doc-tor, said, "Could you help me please."

I went to the doc - tor, said, "Could you help me

please." He said, "Son there ain't no cure 'cause the

blues is your dis-ease."

Rather than play the chords, play
the notes in these two measures.

Fingerpicking Summary

Written below are all of the fingerpick patterns for 4/4 and 3/4 which have been presented so far. They can be used to play literally thousands of songs. Hold any of the 6-, 5-, and 4-string chords and review these patterns – then apply them to songs from sheet music or song books.

Pattern No. 1 for 4/4

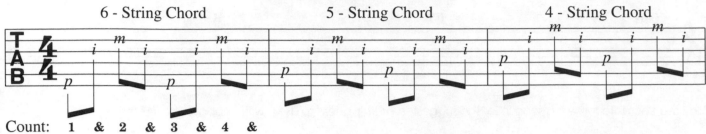

Pattern No. 2 for 4/4

Pattern No. 3 for 4/4 (Travis Picking)

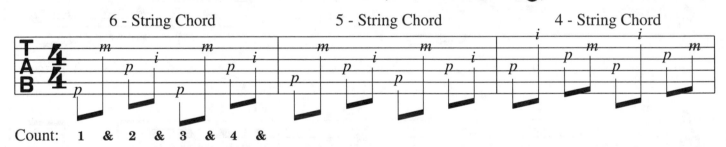

Pattern No. 4 for 4/4 (Travis Variation)

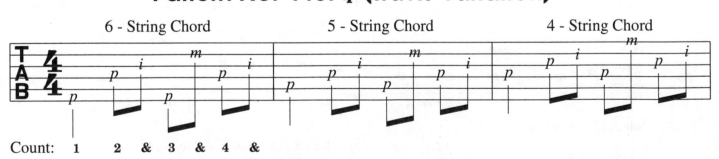

Pattern No. 1 for 3/4

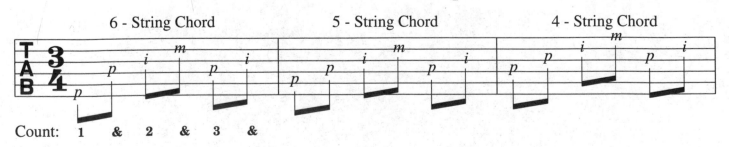

Additional Chords in the Key of D

Drawn below are some commonly used chords in the key of D. These chords are additional to the chords in the key of D which were presented earlier in this book. Learn these chords and practice the following exercises. Use strum and/or fingerpick patterns of your choice. The exercises contain these new chords as well as chords in the key of D which should already have been learned.

Dmaj7
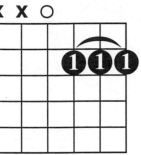

D9
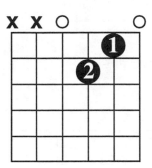

Dadd9
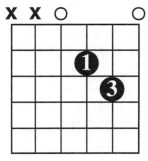

Dsus
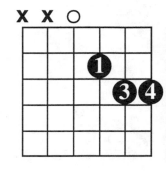

Daug
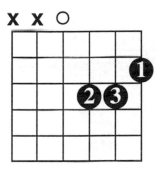

F#m7
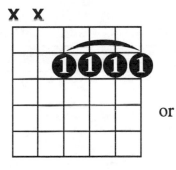

or

F#m7
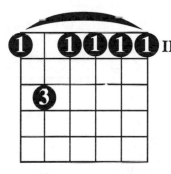

A7sus
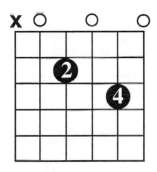

A9
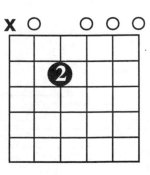

Bm7
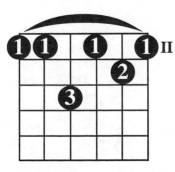

C#dim
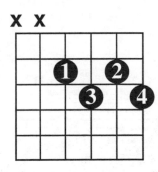

Additional chords in the Key of D

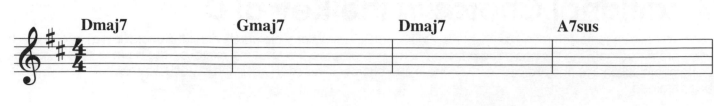

Dmaj7 | Gmaj7 | Dmaj7 | A7sus

Em7 | A9 | A7 | Dmaj7

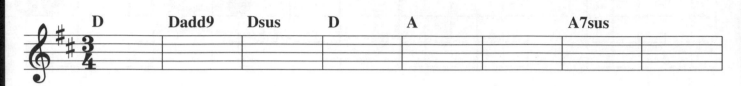

D Dadd9 Dsus | D | A | A7sus

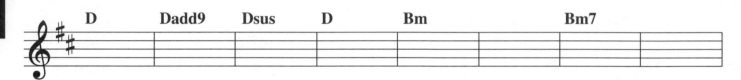

D Dadd9 Dsus | D | Bm | Bm7

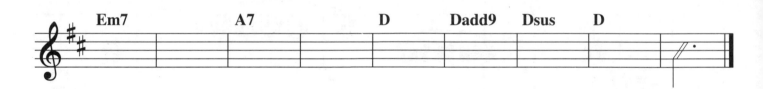

Em7 | A7 | D Dadd9 Dsus | D

D | Daug | G | Gm | D | A7

F#m7 | B7 | Em7 | A7sus A7 | D

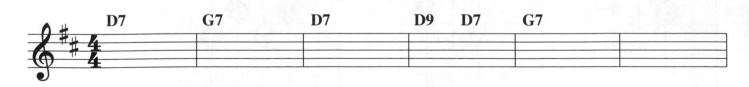

D7 | G7 | D7 | D9 D7 G7 |

D7 | B7 | Em7 | A7 | D

A Minor Pentatonic Scale

Drawn at right is the **A minor pentatonic scale.** This scale can be used to play solos over **Am** and **A7** chords. It can also be used to play blues solos in the **key of A.**

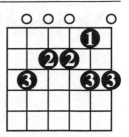

The following two patterns are **minor pentatonic scales** with roots (notes which name the scale) on the fifth string. These two patterns can be moved up the neck and will be used in later solos in the *Mastering the Guitar* method.

CD #2
Track #64

Flatpick Solo
Moderately slow

Long Neck Groove

WB

Diminished Chords

Drawn below are three forms of the diminished chord (also referred to as diminished seventh chord). **Diminished chords** can be written as **"dim"** or with a small circle (**○**) next to the chord name. Diminished chords are unique in that each note in the chord can be the root. *Root* refers to the note which names the scale or chord. For example, the root of a G major chord is G, and the root of a D scale is D. In diminished chords, the letter name of each note fingered can be the letter name of the chord. In a way, the diminished chord fingering is four chords in one. The reason for learning three forms is so chord changes can be more convenient.

Practice these chord forms and play the following exercises.

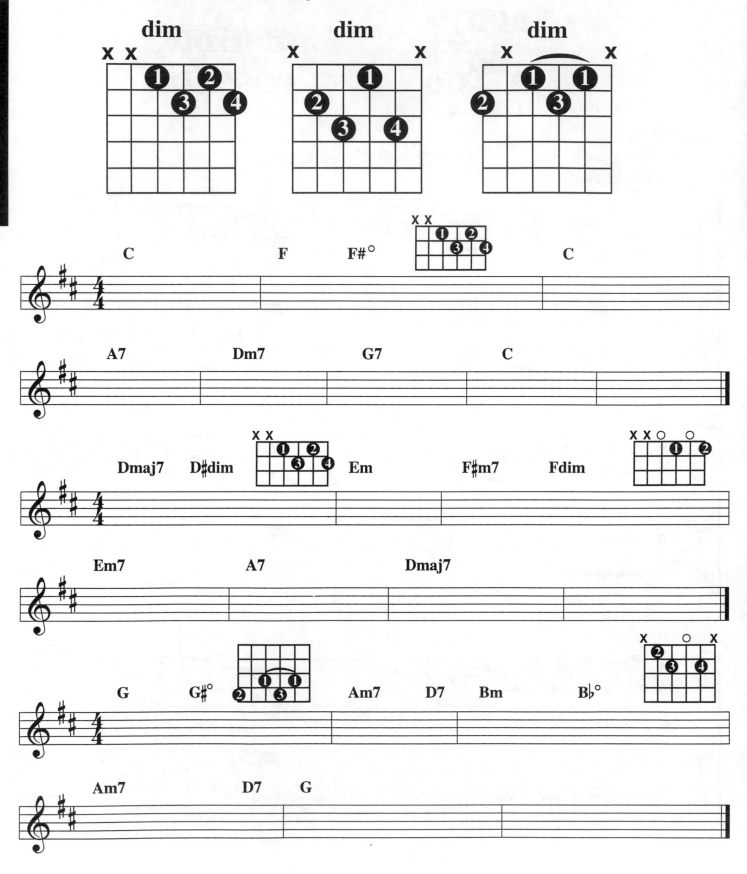

Augmented Chords

Like the diminished chord, each note in the augmented chord can be the root. So, one augmented chord fingering can be three different chords. **Augmented chords** may be written **"aug"** or with a small plus sign (**+**) next to the letter name. Three patterns for augmented chords are drawn below. Again, knowing three forms will help make chord changes convenient.

Practice these chord forms and the following exercises.

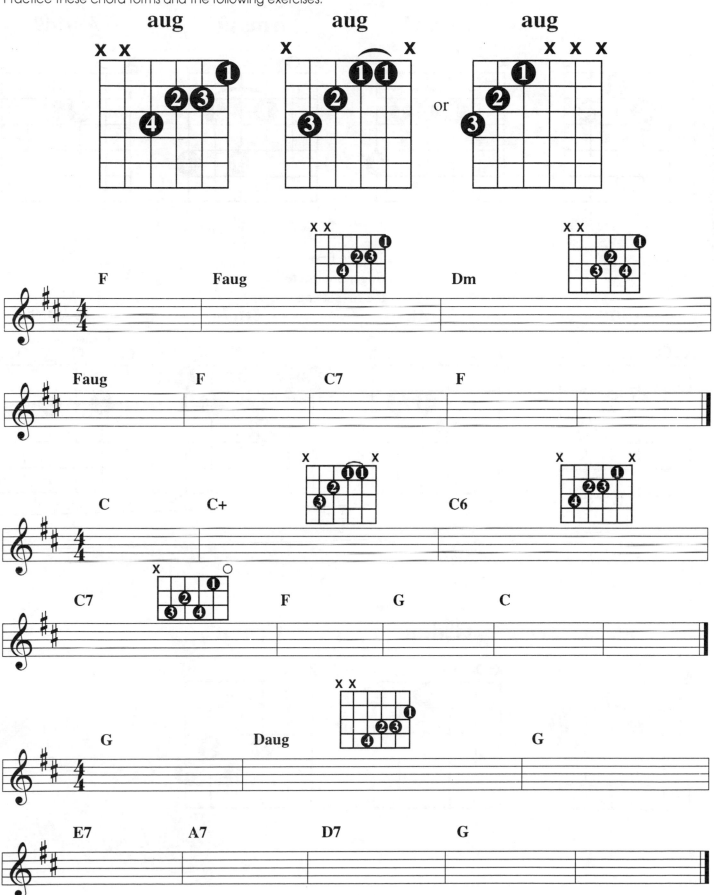

Additional Chords in the Key of A

Drawn below are some commonly used chords in the **key of A.** These chords are additional to the chords in the key of A which were presented earlier in this book. Learn these chords and practice the exercises which follow. Use strum and/or fingerpick patterns of your choice. The exercises contain these new chords as well as chords in the key of A which should have already been learned.

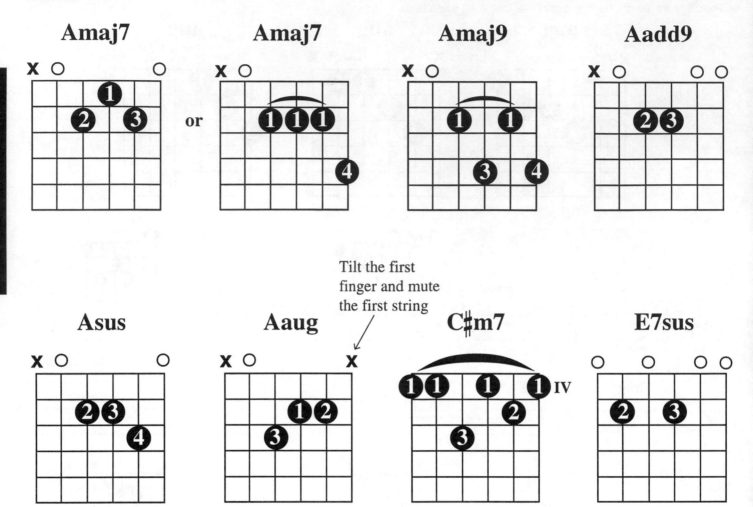

Tilt the first finger and mute the first string

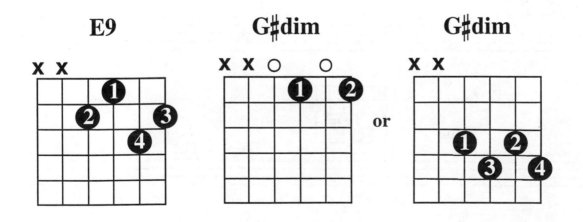

Additional chords in the Key of A

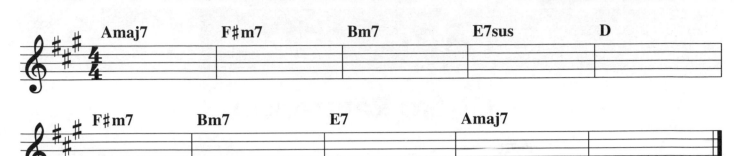

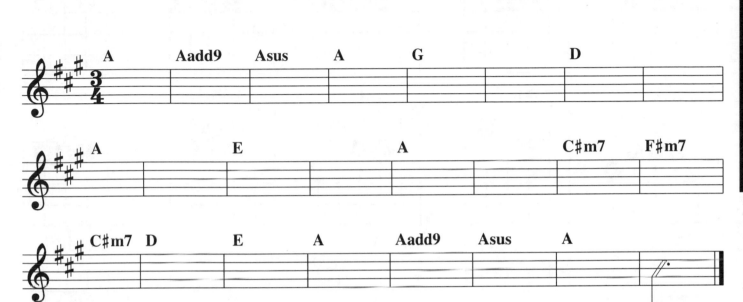

Additional chords in the Key of A

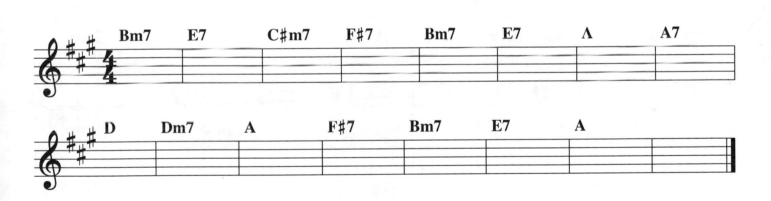

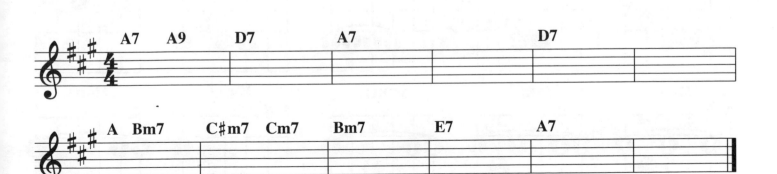

Appendix

Chord Reference

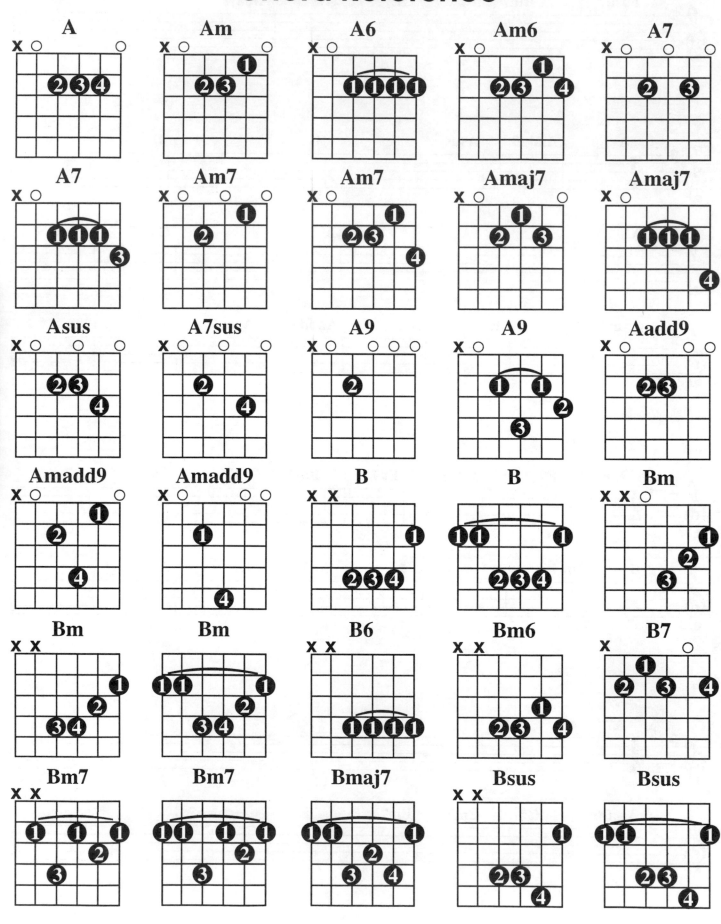

Chord Reference Cont.

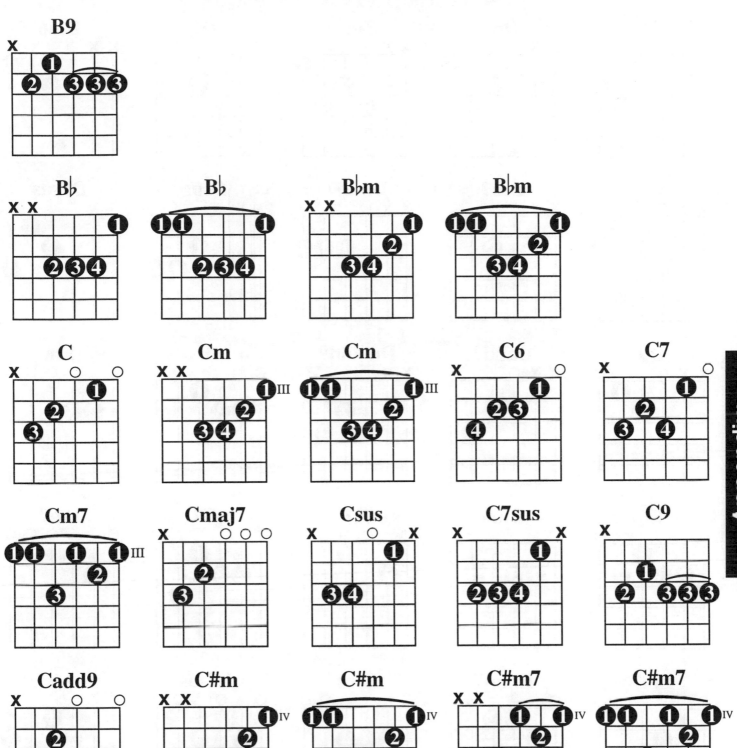

Chord Reference Cont.

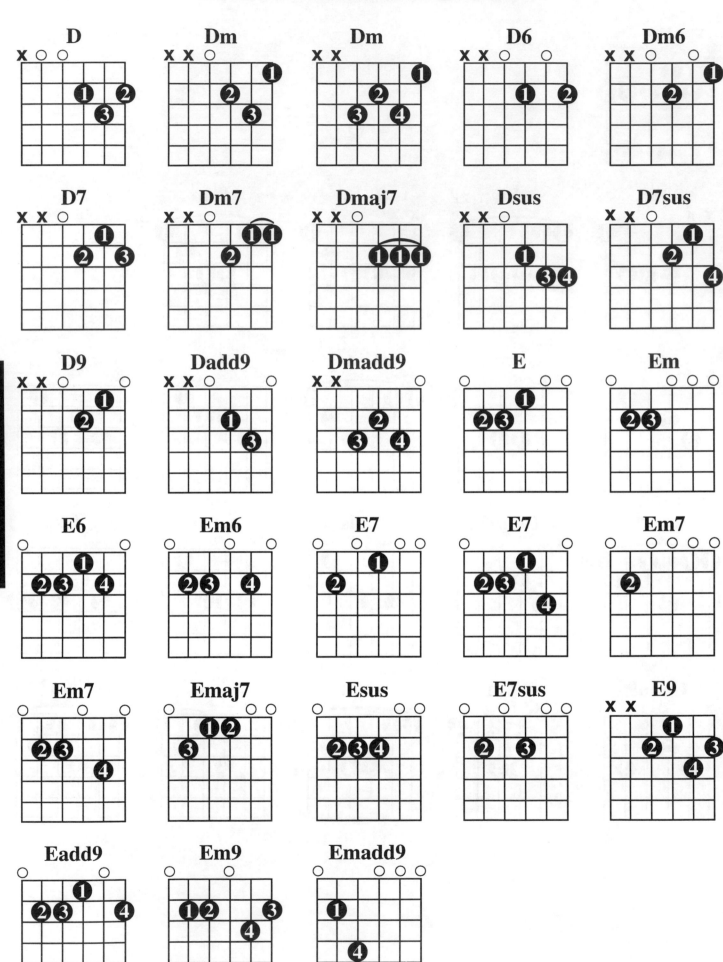

Chord Reference Cont.

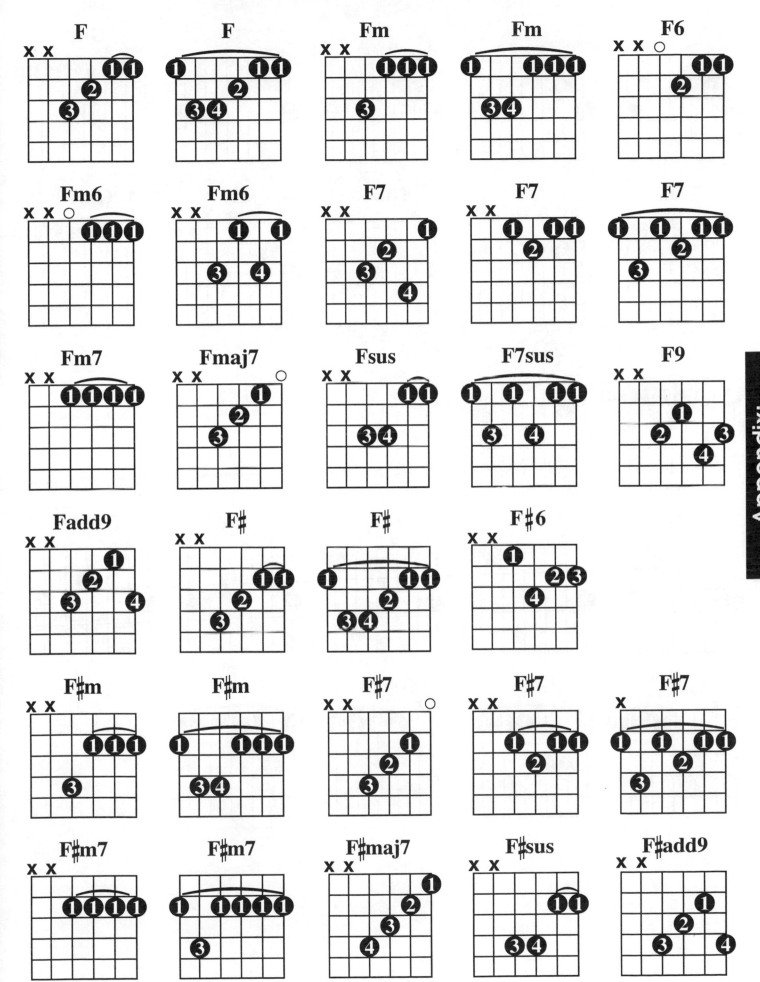

Chord Reference Cont.

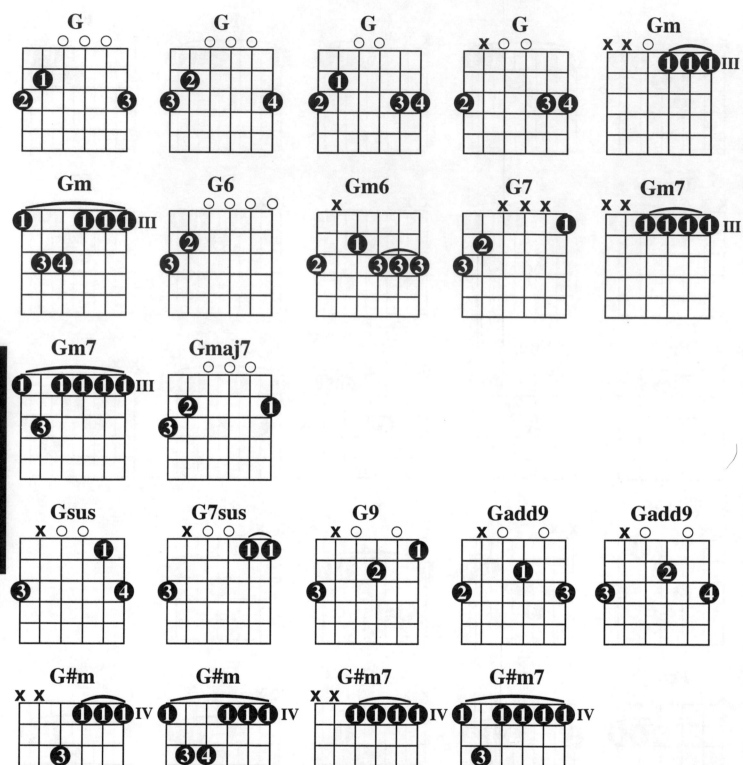

Chord Reference Cont.

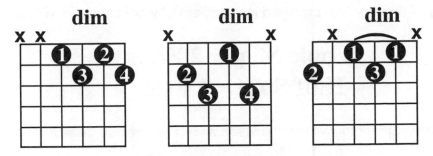

The **diminished seventh chord** can have four letter names for one fingering. Every finger in the pattern is on a note which can be the root (note which names the chord).

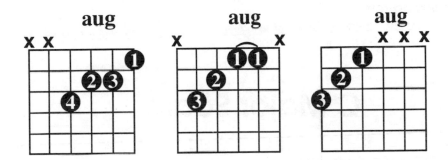

The **augmented chord** can have three letter names for one fingering. Like the diminished chord, each note in the chord can be the root.

Major Scales

A *major scale* is a series of eight notes arranged in a pattern of whole steps and half steps.

Whole Step = 2 Frets
Half Step = 1 Fret

To construct a major scale, start with the note which has the letter name of the scale (often referred to as the *root* or the *tonic*) and use the following formula:

Whole Step

Whole Step

Half Step

Whole Step

Whole Step

Whole Step

Half Step

All major scales must fit this pattern.

The C major scale is shown below with the major scale formula.

C Major Scale

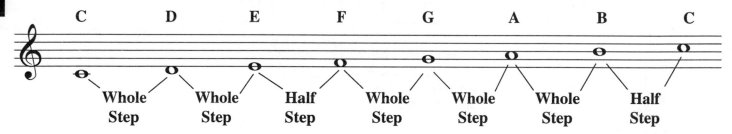

To construct a G scale, the same formula for building major scales is used. Notice that the F is sharp because E to F is only a half step, and the major scale formula requires that particular place in the scale (between the 6th and 7th steps) to be a whole step. In order to establish a whole step between E and F, the F must be sharp.

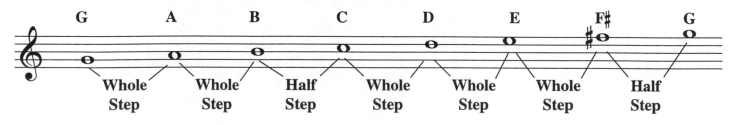

B♭ Major Scale

The B♭ major scale is drawn below. Notice the B is flat (because that is the name of the scale (the root)), and the E is flat. The flats are added so the formula for the major scale will work.

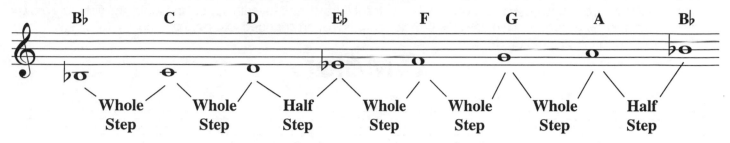

Using the formula for constructing the major scale, on the staves below, build the following major scales. Add sharps or flats to make the formula work.

Appendix: Major Scales

Minor Scales

There are several types of minor scales. The first minor type scale to be built will be the **natural minor.** Natural minor scales are constructed by taking a major scale and lowering (1/2 step) the third, sixth and seventh steps of the scale. The first scale drawn below is C major. In the second scale below, the C major scale has been changed to C natural minor by lowering the third (E), the sixth (A), and the seventh (B) steps.

C Major

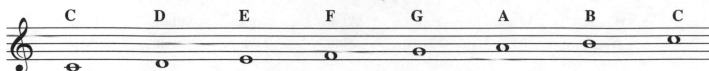

C Natural Minor

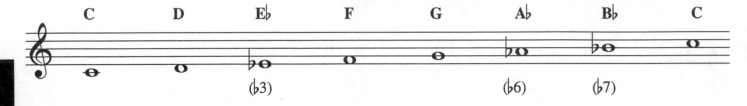

The first scale drawn below is the A major and the second is A natural minor. To lower the third, sixth, and seventh degrees of the A major scale requires omitting the sharps. Notice the A natural minor scale has no sharps or flats. These are the same notes contained in a C major scale. The only difference is A natural minor begins on A and C major begins on C. These to scales are *related.* A minor is the relative minor of C major, and C major is the relative major of A minor. Every minor has its relative major and vice versa. Relative major and minor will be discussed in later books of the **Mastering the Guitar** method.

A Major

A Natural Minor

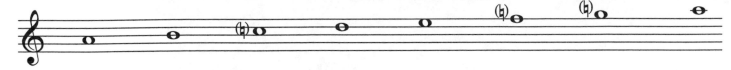

On the staves below, build the natural minor scales indicated. Build the major scales first, and then lower the third, sixth, and seventh degree to make them natural minor scales.

The next type of minor scale to be learned is the **harmonic minor.** The harmonic minor scale is the same as the natural minor except the seventh step of the scale is raised ¹/₂ step. For example, the first scale drawn below is the A natural minor. The second scale below is the A harmonic minor. Notice, the seventh step of the scale (G) has been raised ¹/₂ step (G#). With the harmonic minor scale, the seventh step of the scale (also referred to as the seventh *degree* of the scale) is raised whether the scale is ascending or descending.

A Natural Minor

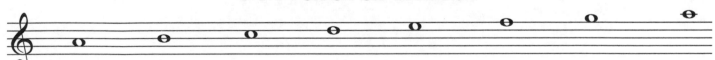

A Harmonic Minor

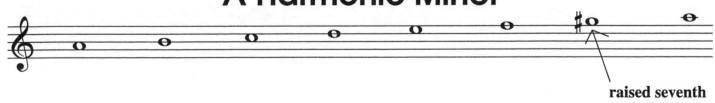

raised seventh

Appendix: Minor Scales

Identifying Key Signatures

You can determine the key of a piece, by looking at the key signature. Remember, the key signature is the sharps or flats which are written at the beginning of each staff. If there are no sharps or flats written, the music is in the key of C (minor keys will be presented later). If there are sharps in the key signature, the name of the key can be determined by going ¹/₂ step (one fret) above the name of the last sharp sign. The last sharp sign being the one furthest to the right. For example, the following is the key signature for the key of A, because the last sharp sign is G♯ and ¹/₂ step above G♯ is A.

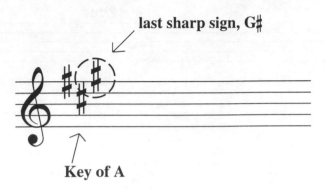

If a piece of music has one flat in the key signature, it is in the **key of "F."** Flat keys can be identified by looking at the next to the last flat sign (the last flat sign being the one to the far right). The name of that flat will be the name of the key. For example, the key signature below is for the key of E♭, because the next to the last flat sign is E♭.

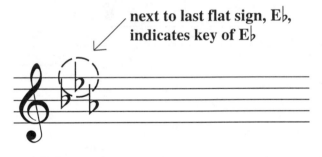

Identify the following keys by the key signatures.

Circle Of Fifths

The diagram below is called a **circle of fifths.** It is named this because, moving clockwise, each letter name is five steps up the major scale from the previous chord. The circle of fifths can be very helpful in finding and remembering key signatures and how many sharps or flats are in each key. The key at the top of the circle, C, has no sharps or flats. The sharp keys are on the right side of the circle and the flat keys are on the left side. Moving clockwise, one more sharp is added to each key. Moving counterclockwise one more flat is added to each key. Written in parenthesis next to each key, are the number of sharps or flats in the key signature for that particular key.

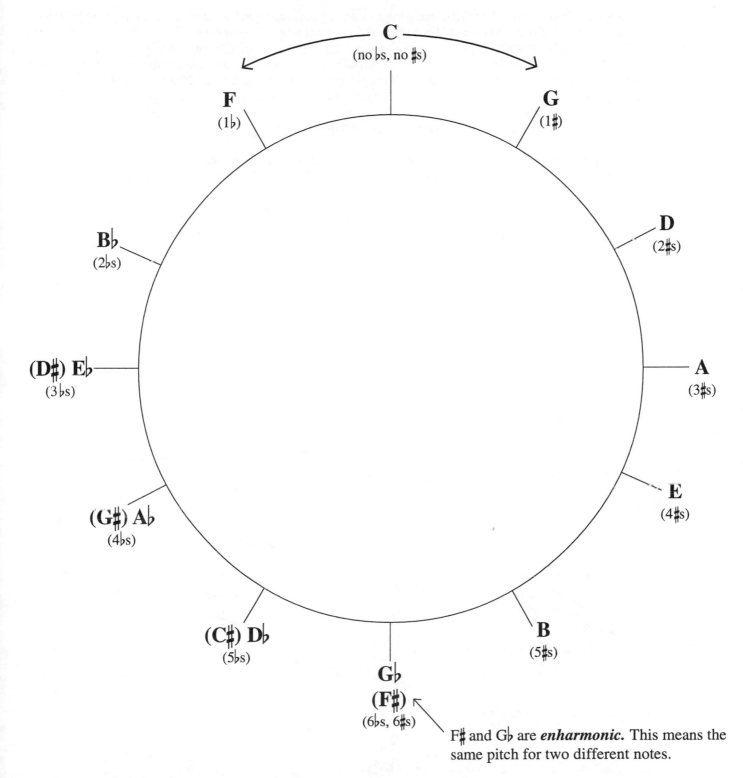

F♯ and G♭ are **enharmonic.** This means the same pitch for two different notes.

The saying, "*Go Down And Eat Breakfast Food*" can be used in memorizing the sharp keys in order of how many sharps are in each key. The first letter in each word identifies the keys moving clockwise around the circle. The saying, "*Funny Big Elephants Always Dance Goofy*" can be used to remember the order of the flat keys moving counterclockwise on the circle.

Transposing

To *transpose* a song means to change the key. Transposing a song may be necessary if the original melody is too high or low for you to sing. Another reason to transpose a piece is that the chords may be too difficult to play in the original key. Transposing the song can simplify the chords. For example, if the original song is in the key of B♭ and the chords to the song are B♭, E♭, Cm7, and F7, the music could be transpose into the key of G and the chords would all become simpler.

The circle of fifths can be used to transpose music by following the steps written below:

1. **Change the letter name of the first chord in the piece to one of the simple key chords. Or, change the first chord to a chord which sounds like it will be better for your vocal range.** For example, if the first chord in the song is B♭, you could change it to G. The easiest keys for the guitar in order of difficulty are: G, C, D, A, E, and F. The easiest minor keys are: Em, Am, Dm, and Bm. Minor chords cannot be changed to major chords and vice versa. However, chords may be simplified. If you are transposing a chord which sounds difficult to play or you do not know, such as F13-9, the chord name may be reduced to F7, or even F if necessary. For example, Dmaj7 can be reduced to a D chord, Em9 can be reduced to Em, and a G13-9 could be reduced to G7. Chords which have names larger than 7 can be reduced to 7th chords.

2. **On the circle of fifths, find the letter name of the original first chord of the song.** Notice, you are locating only the letter name of the chord. Don't be concerned with the type of chord (i.e. m, maj7, 9, sus, etc.).

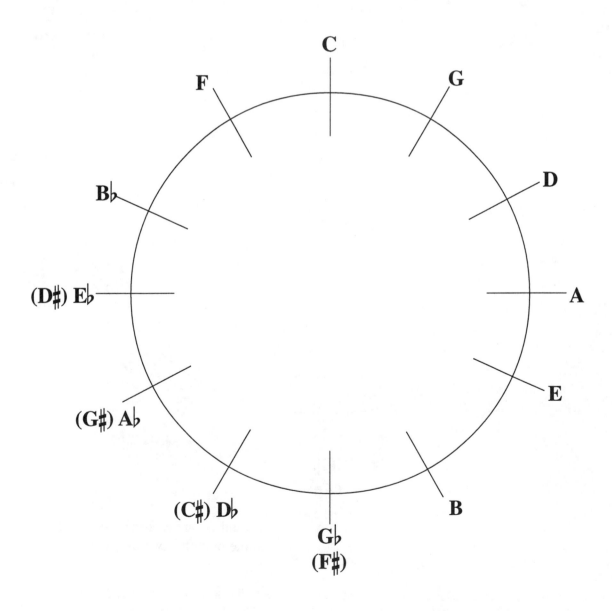

3. **Find, on the clock, the letter name of the new first chord (new key).** This is the new first chord you have selected. The chord is your choice. You may want to keep it simple and easy to sing with. For example, if the first chord in the original music is B♭ and you want to change it to G, the location of these chords is shown on the circle of fifths drawn below.

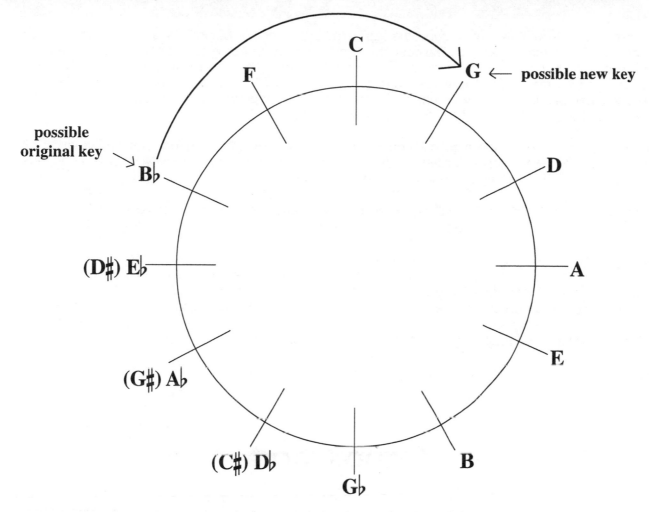

4. **See which direction (clockwise or counterclockwise, which ever is shortest) and how far you moved on the circle to go from the original first chord to the new (better) chord.** For example, if B♭ is being changed to G, G is three chords clockwise on the circle from B♭ (as shown on the clock above).

5. **Change the letter names of the rest of the chords in the piece the same direction and distance as the first chord was changed.** Use only the letter names of the chords to find the changes. The rest of the chord name (i.e. m, m7, maj7, sus, dim, etc.) can be added back to the letter name of the chord after the change has been made. Remember, you cannot change minor chords to major and vice versa. Also, diminished and augmented chords have to remain diminished and augmented. Other chords may be reduced if necessary.

In the example below, the music was originally in the key of B♭ (chords written on the bottom). The music has been transposed into key the of G (chords written on the top). Notice, some of the chords have been simplified after they were transposed. As you can see the top chords would be much easier to play. If the new key, G, is difficult to sing, you may want to transpose the music again into another of the easy keys until you find the one which is comfortable.

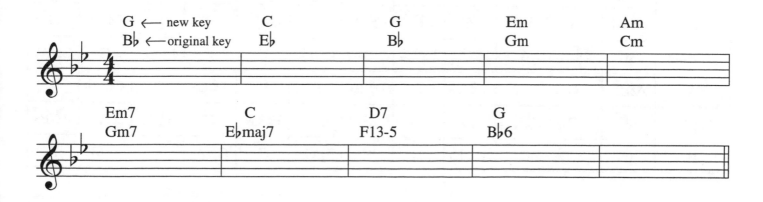

The Capo

Another way to transpose music is to use a *capo.* The capo is a clamp which can be positioned on the guitar neck so that in effect it "shortens" the length of the strings. The capo should be attached just slightly behind and next to the fretwire. When the capo is placed in a particular fret, the notes and chords are fingered as though the fret just above the capo was the first fret. Each fret the capo is moved up will raise the pitch of the chords $1/2$ step. For example, if the capo is placed in the first fret and an Em chord is fingered, the chord will sound like Fm. However, most people who use the capo think in terms of what the chord looks like, rather than what the pitch is that is actually sounding.

A nice feature of using the capo is that a guitarist can play the chords or the melody to a piece and, by correctly positioning the capo, change the key without changing the chords or notes. This can be extremely valuable when accompanying singers or players who play the tune in a key other than the one you are used to.

Using a capo can give a different tonal quality to familiar chords. For example, playing a G chord with the capo in the third fret (which will now sound like B♭) will give the G chord a different sound than it had without using the capo.

The following chart shows the relationships of the chord which is fingered to the resulting pitch of the chord when the capo is used. Simply match the chord you want to hear with the chord you want to finger, and place the capo accordingly. Chords are listed with their enharmonic names. For example, an A♯ chord can also be referred to a B♭ chord. Any chord type with the same letter name can be used. For example, C could be used for C7, Cm, C9, Cdim, and any type of C chord.

It is unlikely the capo would be used any higher than the seventh or eighth fret.

Capo Chart

Capo on   *Actual Sound of Chord*

Chord held

Fret #	1	2	3	4	5	6	7	8	9	10	11	12
C	C♯/D♭	D	D♯/E♭	E	F	F♯/G♭	G	G♯/A♭	A	A♯/B♭	B	C
C♯/D♭	D	D♯/E♭	E	F	F♯/G♭	G	G♯/A♭	A	A♯/B♭	B	C	C♯/D♭
D	D♯/E♭	E	F	F♯/G♭	G	G♯/A♭	A	A♯/B♭	B	C	C♯/D♭	D
D♯/E♭	E	F	F♯/G♭	G	G♯/A♭	A	A♯/B♭	B	C	C♯/D♭	D	D♯/E♭
E	F	F♯/G♭	G	G♯/A♭	A	A♯/B♭	B	C	C♯/D♭	D	D♯/E♭	E
F	F♯/G♭	G	G♯/A♭	A	A♯/B♭	B	C	C♯/D♭	D	D♯/E♭	E	F
F♯/G♭	G	G♯/A♭	A	A♯/B♭	B	C	C♯/D♭	D	D♯/E♭	E	F	F♯/G♭
G	G♯/A♭	A	A♯/B♭	B	C	C♯/D♭	D	D♯/E♭	E	F	F♯/G♭	G
G♯/A♭	A	A♯/B♭	B	C	C♯/D♭	D	D♯/E♭	E	F	F♯/G♭	G	G♯/A♭
A	A♯/B♭	B	C	C♯/D♭	D	D♯/E♭	E	F	F♯/G♭	G	G♯/A♭	A
A♯/B♭	B	C	C♯/D♭	D	D♯/E♭	E	F	F♯/G♭	G	G♯/A♭	A	A♯/B♭
B	C	C♯/D♭	D	D♯/E♭	E	F	F♯/G♭	G	G♯/A♭	A	A♯/B♭	B